Fast Facts on Bible Prophecy

THOMAS ICE & TIMOTHY DEMY

HARVEST HOUSE PUBLISHERS
Eugene, Oregon 97402

Except where otherwise indicated, Scripture quotations in this book are taken from the New American Standard Bible, ©1960, 1962, 1963, 1968, 1971, 1972, 1973, 1975, 1977 by The Lockman Foundation. Used by permission.

Scripture quotations marked KJV are taken from the Kings James Version of the Bible.

FAST FACTS ON BIBLE PROPHECY
Copyright ©1997 by Pre-Trib Research Center
Published by Harvest House Publishers
Eugene, Oregon 97402

Library of Congress Cataloging-in-Publication Data

Ice, Thomas.
    Fast facts on Bible prophecy / Thomas Ice and Timothy Demy.
       p. cm.
    Includes bibliographical references and index.
    ISBN 1-56507-665-6
    1. Bible—Prophecies—Terminology. 2. Prophecy—Christianity—Terminology.
I. Demy, Timothy J. II. Title.
BS647.2.I24   1997
220.1'5'03—dc21   97-7444
                                                        CIP

Printed in the United States of America.

97 98 99 00 01 02 03 /BP/ 10 9 8 7 6 5 4 3 2 1

To Doctors John and Constance Vitaliti
who have a great desire to
know Christ and His Word
and to see His soon return

INTRODUCTION

Every area of study, every profession, every vocation, every discipline has its own vocabulary that is used to define concepts, clarify differences, and provide a common means of dialogue. It doesn't matter if you are studying medicine or mechanical engineering, law or languages, nutrition or nursing, computers or chemistry, technology or theology. They all use specialized terms and concepts that can bewilder beginning students and readers. It is impossible to think deeply on any subject without precise and technical language to guide us. But vocabulary *can* be learned if a person believes there is some purpose or benefit in it. Certainly knowledge of God's Word and the truths it contains are worthy of our time and efforts!

The confusion regarding prophetic terms is unfortunate because it causes many people to discard or denigrate the study of Bible prophecy—and God's Word was written to be studied and understood. But exploring any new area of study requires learning new terminology. Most of us don't shy away from using a computer even though we can't fully explain "megabyte" or "modem."

Fast Facts on Bible Prophecy gives a summary of important words and phrases to help you gain a better understanding of biblical prophecy. The topics are presented alphabetically, and charts accompany many of the entries to help you visualize the concepts. (Didn't someone once say "a picture is worth a thousand words"!)

We encourage you to browse the book, reading about terms that are unfamiliar or reviewing the ones that are familiar. We hope you will find this book "fast" and "factual" so you will keep it handy and not be afraid to use it.

The theological perspective throughout the book is that of premillennialism and pretribulationism. Although we recognize that this is not the only position embraced by evangelical Christians, we believe it is the most widely held perspective. It is also our conviction that premillennialism, specifically pretribulationism, *best* explains the prophetic plan of God as revealed in the Bible.

This book is designed to be a ready reference, a source for quick overviews and fast facts. We have not engaged in lengthy discussions or debates of opposing perspectives, but have tried to provide concise presentations from our own tradition. The bibliography provides ample resources for those who desire to dig deeper or engage in the finer details of the topics covered.

Throughout the book, we have relied heavily upon the thoughts and writings of two individuals: Dr. John F. Walvoord and Dr. Arnold Fruchtenbaum. The writings of these two men reflect decades of studying biblical prophecy and attempting to properly piece together the "prophetic puzzle." They have greatly influenced our own thinking. And often what started as their thoughts became our own so it is sometimes hard to untangle them. Nevertheless we have attempted to give full credit throughout the book for use of their materials (and those of others), and any omissions are unintended and fully our responsibility.

We hope you profit from this volume of information. As you read, don't forget that Christ could return at any moment to take us home. Maranatha!

Abaddon

Abaddon is a satanic angel and king of the abyss as revealed in Revelation 9:11. *Abaddon* is the rendering of his name in the Hebrew tongue, while *Apollyon* is his Greek name. Both terms mean "destruction." *Abaddon* is used six times in the Old Testament to connote the place or condition of the wicked in Sheol (Job 26:6; 28:22; 31:12; Psalm 88:11; Proverbs 15:11; 27:20). Consistent with his name, Abaddon and his hoard of demonic locusts are part of the "first woe" (Revelation 9:3-12) and are released around the middle of the tribulation in order to inflict pain (just short of death) on humanity for five months.

See also "Apollyon."

Abomination of Desolation

The abomination of desolation is mentioned in the Bible seven times and refers to both a past (Daniel 11:31) and future event (Daniel 9:27; 12:11; Matthew 24:15; Mark 13:14; 2 Thessalonians 2:3,4; Revelation 13:15). An abomination of desolation was performed by the Seleucid ruler Antiochus IV (Antiochus Epiphanes) in the second century B.C. (175–164), when he sacrificed a pig to Zeus on the altar of the Jewish temple in Jerusalem. This blatant act of religious defilement in God's temple so outraged the Jewish faithful that it became known as "the abomination (that makes) desolate." A detailed account of this event is recorded in the apocryphal book of 1 Maccabees 1:54ff.

This defilement by Antiochus Epiphanes illustrates the future desecration that will occur at the midpoint of the seven-year tribulation in the rebuilt temple in Jerusalem.

Jesus' reference to this is recorded in Matthew 24:15 and Mark 13:4. The event is built upon the Old Testament notion of "abomination," which denotes a hatred of idolatry and a moral abhorrence, especially in light of ceremonial law

A compilation of all the biblical passages yields the following future scenario: A third Jewish temple will be built on the present temple mount, where the Dome of the Rock now stands, within three-and-a-half years of the beginning of the tribulation. At this point, the false prophet (Revelation 13:11-18), acting on behalf of the Antichrist, will set up his image in the Holy of Holies in the rebuilt temple, defiling it and fulfilling the prophecy of abomination of desolation.

The prophetic significance of this act is the clear identification and recognition of the Antichrist to the Jewish nation and the inauguration of his anti-Semitic reign and intense persecution of the Jews. This is why the Jews of Jerusalem and Judea are commanded to "flee to the mountains" when they see this identifying act occur (Matthew 24:16).

Abrahamic Covenant

The Abrahamic covenant is the "mother" of the redemptive covenants, and all of God's spiritual blessings for mankind spring forth from it. (See Genesis 12:1-3,7; 13:14-17; 15:1-21; 17:1-21; 22:15-18.) This covenant is a pivotal issue in Bible prophecy regarding whether it is still in force for national Israel. Dr. Arnold Fruchtenbaum tells us that the Abrahamic covenant is an "unconditional covenant [that] can be defined as a sovereign act of God whereby God unconditionally obligates Himself to bring to pass definite promises, blessings, and conditions for the covenanted people. It is a unilateral covenant. This type of covenant is characterized by the formula 'I will' which declares God's determination to do

Abrahamic Covenant

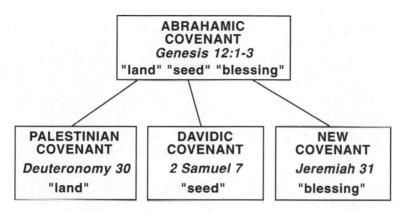

exactly as He promised. The blessings are secured by the grace of God" (*Israelology*, p. 570).

The three major provisions of the Abrahamic covenant revolve around the promise of a land, a seed, and a world-wide blessing (Genesis 12:1-3). While Abraham and his physical descendants—Israel—are the major parties of the covenant, the Gentiles are also included as participants. The covenant can be divided further into the following 14 stipulations (taken from Genesis):

1. A great *nation* was to come out of Abraham, namely, the nation of Israel (12:2; 13:16; 15:5; 17:1,2,7; 22:17).
2. He was promised a land specifically, the *land* of Canaan (12:1,5-7; 13:14,15,17; 15:18-21; 17:8).
3. *Abraham* himself was to be greatly blessed (12:2; 15:6; 22:15-17).
4. Abraham's *name* would be great (12:2).
5. Abraham will be a *blessing* to others (12:2).

6. Those who bless will be *blessed* (12:3).
7. Those who curse will be *cursed* (12:3).
8. In Abraham everyone will ultimately be blessed since there's a promise of *Gentile* blessing (12:3; 22:18).
9. Abraham would receive a *son* through his wife, Sarah (15:1-4; 17:16-21).
10. His descendants would undergo the Egyptian *bondage* (15:13,14).
11. Other *nations,* as well as Israel, would come forth from Abraham (17:3,4,6); (the Arab states are some of these nations).
12. His name would be changed from Abram to *Abraham* (17:5).
13. Sarai's name was to be changed to *Sarah* (17:15).
14. There was to be a token of the covenant—*circumcision* (17:9-14). According to the Abrahamic covenant, circumcision was a sign of Jewishness.

(From Fruchtenbaum, *Israelology*, pp. 574–75)

The 14 promises are distributed and fulfilled among the three parties as follows:

1. Abraham—1, 2, 3, 4, 5, 6, 9, 11, 12, 13
2. Israel, the seed—1, 2, 5, 6, 7, 10, 14
3. Gentiles—6, 7, 8, 11

The significance of the Abrahamic covenant for Bible prophecy relates to one's understanding of how God is fulfilling the promises. All believe that Christ facilitates fulfillment of many aspects of the covenant (Galatians 3:6–4:11). Amillennialists, postmillennialists, and covenant theology adherents generally believe that the church takes over all the promises, while national Israel has been disenfranchised. Premillennialists generally believe that the church partakes in the spiritual blessings of the covenant (Romans 15:27; Galatians 3:6-29). They conclude that in the future Israel will experience fulfillment of her national promises when the nation is regathered and accepts Jesus as the Messiah. Thus, the church is rightly seen as a *partaker* in the promises given through Abraham, not a *supplanter* of those stipulations destined for fulfillment through national Israel. Only a literal fulfillment of all the blessings to Israel, the Gentiles, and the church does justice to God's plan as stated throughout the Bible.

Abyss

Abyss is the English transliteration of the Greek word *abussos* which literally means "boundless," or "bottomless."

See also "Bottomless Pit."

Age

Age comes from the Greek words *aiôn* and *aiônios,* which mean "a period of time," whether past, present, or future. The Bible sometimes speaks of periods of history and eternity as ages. Ages are similar to dispensations, but differ in emphasis. *Ages* stress the period of *time,* while dispensations focus on the *nature* of a period. Therefore references to future ages provide information useful for understanding Bible prophecy. Scripture speaks of the following ages:

- before the ages—before the beginning of time in eternity past (1 Corinthians 2:7)
- past ages—the periods of time before Christ's first coming (Ephesians 3:5; Colossians 1:26)

- this age—the current time period in which we live (between the two comings of Christ) (Galatians 1:4; Ephesians 1:21)
- ages to come—the remaining time periods since the first coming of Christ (Ephesians 2:7). This would include the millennium and eternity

Amillennialism

One of the three major views of Bible prophecy (the others are premillennialism and postmillennialism). According to amillennialism, there will be no literal, future 1000-year reign of Christ on earth; however, it usually holds that there is a present spiritual form of the kingdom. The English theological term is made up of the following elements: *a* is from the Greek and means "no." *Mille* and *annus* are Latin and mean "thousand" and "years" respectively. Thus, amillennialism means "no thousand years."

Amillennialism teaches that from the ascension of Christ in the first century until His second coming both good and evil will increase in the world as God's kingdom parallels Satan's kingdom. (There is no rapture.) Even though it believes that Satan is currently bound, it teaches that evil increases. When Jesus Christ returns, the end of the world will occur with a general resurrection and general judgment of all people. This view is essentially a spiritualization of the kingdom prophecies.

Amillennialism was not present in the earliest church; at least there is no positive record of its existence. It appears to have risen first as a result of opposition to premillennial literalism and then later, developed into a positive system. Amillennialism came to dominate the church when the great church father and theologian Augustine (354–430) abandoned premillennialism in favor of amillennialism. It is no

AMILLENNIALISM

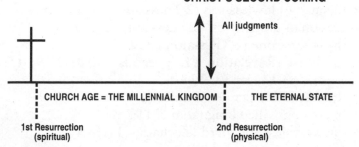

CHRIST'S SECOND COMING

All judgments

CHURCH AGE = THE MILLENNIAL KINGDOM   THE ETERNAL STATE

1st Resurrection
(spiritual)

2nd Resurrection
(physical)

exaggeration to say that among the church's leadership (including the majority of protestant reformers during the fifteenth and sixteenth centuries) amillennialism has been the most widely held view for much of the church's history.

Antichrist

The Antichrist is the individual who arises during the tribulation and gains worldwide power for three-and-a-half years. He is the imitator of the program of Jesus Christ and is known by many names throughout the Bible. The Antichrist is discussed extensively in many Bible passages.

Except for 1 John 2:22, the Bible never specifically refers to this coming leader as "the Antichrist." It is a term that has been used by students of prophecy throughout church history to refer to him. The title "Antichrist" is clearly an appropriate term for it captures the essence of the person and his work against God. Among his many identifications are the following:

- the little horn (Daniel 7:8)
- the insolent king (Daniel 8:23)

- the prince who is to come (Daniel 9:26)
- the one who makes desolate; the abomination of desolation (Daniel 9:27; Matthew 24:15)
- the man of lawlessness (2 Thessalonians 2:3)
- the son of destruction (2 Thessalonians 2:3)
- the lawless one (2 Thessalonians 2:8)
- the beast (Revelation 11:7; see also 13:1; 14:9; 15:2; 16:2; 17:3,13; 19:20; 20:10)
- the despicable person (Daniel 11:21)
- the strong-willed king (Daniel 11:36)
- the worthless shepherd (Zechariah 11:16,17)

According to Daniel 9:27, the Antichrist will emerge in power during the prophetic milestone known as the "seventieth week," after the fulfillment of the previously prophesied "69 weeks." After Christ returns and removes the church from the earth, the Antichrist will ascend to power and, as the "little horn" spoken of in Daniel 7:24,25, will lead a confederation of western powers during the tribulation years. The Antichrist's future reign is certain, but it will not commence until after the rapture occurs and the tribulation begins.

Two words describe the ascent of the Antichrist: *unification* and *subjugation*. According to Daniel 7:7,8 and 7:23,24, the Antichrist will rise to power after the confederation of ten nations emerges. This confederation is symbolized as a beast with ten horns and represents a final international political entity. It will be a unique and powerful empire. According to Daniel, "The fourth beast will be a fourth kingdom on the earth, which will be different from all the other kingdoms and it will devour the whole earth and tread it down and crush it" (7:23).

The Antichrist will forcibly take control of the confederation and will subdue three of the ten members. "As for the ten horns, out of this kingdom ten kings will arise; and another will arise after them, and he will be different from the previous ones and will subdue three kings" (7:24). John writes of the Antichrist's ascent in Revelation 13:1: "And he stood on the sand of the seashore. And I saw a beast coming up out of the sea, having ten horns and seven heads, and on his horns were ten diadems, and on his heads were blasphemous names."

While the Antichrist emerges in a political environment and functions initially as a political leader, he will gradually acquire religious connotations. Eventually he will require those subject to him to worship him when he sets up his image in Israel's temple (2 Thessalonians 2:4).

The Antichrist will be a leader who pursues peace and wages war. In his pursuit of peace he will be both successful and deceitful; in his waging of war he will be daring and destructive. The Antichrist is often portrayed in the Bible as a warrior.

Once the Antichrist is in power and his program is fully manifested, it will be all encompassing and intense. He will be active throughout all of the tribulation, but it is primarily the last half that will be tumultuous. His unprecedented, unparalleled, and unrestrained power will command worldwide attention for 42 months.

For three-and-a-half years, the Antichrist will persecute Christians and other opponents in a reign of terror that will dwarf all suffering and death experienced by humanity in previous persecutions, plagues, and pogroms. Once his mask as a man of peace is removed, "the lawless one" will be revealed as a man of terror. This fits the historic pattern of satanic deception, which presents evil as good, lies as truth, and wickedness as righteousness.

According to the Bible, great armies from the east and the west will gather. The Antichrist will deal with threats to his power from the south, and he will also move to destroy a revived Babylon in the east. Then he will finally turn his forces toward Jerusalem to subdue and destroy it. As they move on Jerusalem, God will intervene and Jesus Christ will return. The Lord will destroy the armies, capture the Antichrist and the False Prophet, and cast them into the lake of fire (Revelation 19:11-21).

When the Lord returns, the power and rule of the Antichrist will come to an end at the campaign of Armageddon. The second coming of Christ will crush the Antichrist and his armies and will bring forth a time of judgment (Revelation 19:20,21). The Antichrist will be finished in history (unlike Satan who will be bound for 1000 years and then released and judged after a final rebellion [see Revelation 20:10]). In all of his actions and attitudes, the Antichrist will indeed be *against* Christ, but it will be Christ—not his human enemy—who will have the final victory. The judgment of Antichrist immediately precedes the binding of Satan and the inauguration of the millennial reign of Christ on earth.

See also "Antichrist, Nationality of."

Antichrist, Nationality of

A widely-held belief throughout the history of the church has been the notion that Antichrist will be of Jewish origin. Upon closer examination, there is no real scriptural basis for such a view.

Arguments for Jewish Origin   Three reasons are often given in support of the argument that Antichrist will be Jewish. First, it is argued that he will be a Jew since the Jews are responsible for the world's problems. Thus, it follows that the greatest problem of history—Antichrist—will also be

Jewish. This is the anti-Semitic reason. Since we do not have enough space to give an in-depth refutation of anti-Semitism, we note that since anti-Semitism is unbiblical so is any logic that reasons upon such a premise.

Dr. Arnold Fruchtenbaum offers a refutation of the second reason, which he calls "The Logical Reason." He writes:

> Stated in a syllogism, this argument goes as follows:
>
> | | |
> |---|---|
> | Major Premise: | The Jews will accept the Antichrist as the Messiah. |
> | Minor Premise: | The Jews will never accept a Gentile as the Messiah. |
> | Conclusion: | The Antichrist will be a Jew. |

The difficulties of this argument are many, not the least of which are the two premises. Neither premise can be supported biblically. Just because the Jews make a covenant with the Antichrist (Daniel 9:26,27), it does not follow either textually or logically that they accept him as messiah (or Antichrist). Second, since they are not accepting him as messiah, the fact that he is a Gentile peacemaker is irrelevant.

An attempt at a scriptural argument reasons that Antichrist will spring forth from the tribe of Dan. Support for this third view is inappropriately derived from Genesis 49:17; Deuteronomy 33:22; Jeremiah 8:16; Daniel 11:37; and Revelation 7:4-8. Even though many passages are cited in support of this argument, none of them actually support the notion since they are all taken out of context. In reality, only Daniel 11:37 refers to the Antichrist. Even though some believe that the phrase in Daniel 11:37, "the God of his fathers" (KJV), implies a Jewish apostasy, the phrase is more accurately translated "the gods of his fathers" (NASB). Since Antichrist will in fact be a Gentile, as will be shown below, the argument is unfounded. Since the original Hebrew supports the NASB translation and not the KJV, Antichrist's apostasy will be Christian and not Jewish. (Much of this material is taken from Fruchtenbaum, "The Nationality of the Anti-Christ".)

Arguments for a Gentile Origin We have seen that the Bible does not teach that Antichrist will be Jewish. However, Scripture does teach that he will be of Gentile descent. This can first be seen from biblical typology. Most commentators agree that Daniel 11 speaks of Antiochus Epiphanes, a Gentile, who typifies the future Antichrist. Since Antiochus is a Gentile, then so will be Antichrist.

Second, biblical imagery supports a Gentile origin of Antichrist. Scripture pictures Antichrist as rising up out of the sea (Revelation 13:1; 17:15). In prophetic literature the sea is an image of the Gentile nations. Thus, Antichrist is seen as a Gentile progeny.

Third, the nature of the "times of the Gentiles" (Luke 21:24) supports a Gentile Antichrist. Fruchtenbaum notes:

> It is agreed by all premillennialists that the period known as the Times of the Gentiles does not end until the second coming of Christ. It is further agreed that the Antichrist is the final ruler of the Times of the Gentiles. . . .
>
> If this is so, how then can a Jew be the last ruler at a time when only Gentiles can have the preeminence? To say the Antichrist is to be a Jew would contradict the very nature of the Time of the Gentiles. ("Nationality")

Finally, the Bible not only teaches that Antichrist will be Gentile, but it also tells us he will be of Roman descent. This is understood from Daniel 9:27, where the one cutting a covenant with Israel is said to represent the revived Roman Empire since it was the Romans who destroyed Jerusalem and the temple in A.D. 70.

See also "Antichrist, Spirit of."

Antichrist, Spirit of

In 1 John 4:3 we read, "and every spirit that does not confess Jesus is not from God; and this is the spirit of the antichrist, of which you have heard that it is coming, and now it is already in the world." Here, the phrase "spirit of the antichrist" refers to false prophets and teachers who were influenced by demons. There have been, are, and will continue to be many false teachers—some influenced by demons.

First John 4:1 says, "Beloved, do not believe every spirit, but test the spirits to see whether they are from God, because many false prophets have gone out into the world." How does a believer "test the spirits"? Testing the spirits is not done through a mystical sense that something is not quite right. Instead, a spirit is tested by evaluating the content of its message by the Word of God. The case cited in 1 John 4 relates to the person of Christ. Thus, those who taught error in this matter were proven to be false prophets or antichrists.

All false teachers distort the Word of God and the person and work of Jesus Christ. As such, they oppose Christ in the same way (though not to the same degree) as the final Antichrist. In the same sense that John the Baptist was a forerunner of Jesus Christ, so are these false teachers forerunners of the Antichrist (Matthew 24:5,24; 1 John 2:18,22; 4:3; 2 John 7). Thus, the "spirit of Antichrist" is currently at work preparing the way for *the* Antichrist and his seven-year career.

Antiochus Epiphanes

Antiochus Epiphanes is the Seleucid king Antiochus IV (215–163 B.C.) of who Daniel prophesied in Daniel 11. He ruled in Palestine from 175–164 B.C. He hated Judaism and attempted to eradicate it by forbidding the Jews from practicing their religion and observing the Sabbath. He set up idolatrous altars and forced the Jews to either offer unclean sacrifices or be killed. He believed himself to be Zeus, and on Chislev 25 (December 16, 167 B.C.) he defiled the temple in Jerusalem by erecting an altar to Zeus on the altar and offered swine's flesh as a burnt offering. He then directed that similar offerings be made monthly. Such defilement or "abomination of desolation" fulfilled Daniel's prophecy and ultimately led to the Maccabean revolution.

Antiochus Epiphanes died insane in 163 B.C. His blatant act, prophesied by Daniel and recorded in the apocryphal book 1 Maccabees, prefigures the similar act of abomination of desolation spoken of by Jesus in Matthew 24:15 and Mark 13:4. According to Revelation 13:11-18, this future event will occur at the midpoint of the tribulation, when the false prophet defiles the temple by setting up an image of the Antichrist in the rebuilt temple and inaugurating three-and-a-half years of intense persecution of the Jews.

See also "Abomination of Desolation."

Apocalypse

Apocalypse is the English transliteration of the Greek word *apokalupsis*, which is the ancient title for the book of Revelation. In the ancient world it was a common practice to entitle a book by the first word in the text. Such is the case with Revelation.

Apollyon

Apollyon (meaning "destruction") is the Greek name of the satanic angel and king of the abyss as mentioned in Revelation 9:11.

See also "Abaddon."

Apostasy

The English meaning of *apostasy* means to depart from one's faith. There are two words used in the Greek New Testament for apostasy. First is *apostasia*, from which we get our English word *apostasy*. The noun *apostasia* is a compound of two Greek words: *apo*, "from," and *istémi*, which means "to stand," hence "to stand away from" or, more smoothly put, "to depart from." Next, is the verb *piptô* which simply means "to fall" or "fall away from." For example, when used abstractly, "falling away from the faith" fits into the category of apostasy.

There are seven major passages that warn of the dangers latent during the church's last days (1 Timothy 4:1-3; 2 Timothy 3:1-5; 4:3,4; James 5:1-8; 2 Peter 2; 3:3-6; Jude 1-25). Interestingly, virtually all of these comments come from the epistles written shortly before the death of each apostle writing (that is, during the last days of the various apostles), as if to highlight their warnings about apostasy in the last days of the current church age. Every one of these passages emphasizes over and over again that the great characteristic of the final time of the church will be that of apostasy.

It is likely that the seventh church (Laodicea) of Revelation chapters 2–3 represents the condition of the final stage of the church. Laodicea is clearly the most apostate of the seven churches. In fact, our Lord threatens to spew this self-sufficient church out of His mouth (Revelation 3:16). The apostasy of the church in our day is preparing Christendom for its role as the "great whore of babylon" (Revelation 17:1-7, KJV), who will be used by the Antichrist to gain world power until the midpoint of the tribulation.

The New Testament pictures the condition within the professing church at the end of the age by a system of denials:

- Denial of *God*—Luke 17:26; 2 Timothy 3:4,5
- Denial of *Christ*—1 John 2:18; 4:3; 2 Peter 2:6
- Denial of *Christ's return*—2 Peter 3:3,4
- Denial of *the faith*—1 Timothy 4:1,2; Jude 3,4
- Denial of *sound doctrine*—2 Timothy 4:3,4
- Denial of *the separated life*—2 Timothy 3:1-7
- Denial of *Christian liberty*—1 Timothy 4:3,4
- Denial of *morals*—2 Timothy 3:1-8,13; Jude 18
- Denial of *authority*—2 Timothy 3:4

(Pentecost, *Things to Come*, p. 155)

Dr. Lewis Sperry Chafer, founder and first president of Dallas Theological Seminary, characterizes the last days apostasy for the church in the following way:

A very extensive body of Scripture bears on the last days for the Church. Reference is to a restricted time at the very end of, and yet wholly within, the present age. Though this brief period immediately precedes the great tribulation and in some measure is a preparation for it, these two times of apostasy and confusion—though incomparable in history—are wholly separate the one from the other. Those Scriptures which set forth the last days for the Church give no consideration to political or world conditions but are confined to the Church itself. These Scriptures picture men as departing from the faith (1 Timothy 4:1-2). There will be a manifestation of characteristics which belong to unregenerate men, though it is under the profession of "a form of godliness" (cf. 2 Timothy 3:1-5). The indication is that, having denied the power of the blood of Christ (cf. 2 Timothy 3:5 with Romans 1:16; 1 Corinthians 1:23-24; 2 Timothy 4:2-4), the leaders in these forms of righteousness will be unregenerate men from whom nothing more spiritual than this could proceed (cf. 1 Corinthians 2:14) (Chafer, *Systematic Theology*, vol. IV, p. 375).

The clear course of the last days for the church consists of constant warnings to the believer to be on guard against doctrinal defection (otherwise known as apostasy). Scripture indicates that apostasy will also characterize Christendom during the time when the rapture will take place. The current church age apostasy is preparation for even greater deception and the "falling away" that will characterize the career of the Antichrist during the tribulation.

Armageddon

Armageddon will be the last great world war of history and will take place in Israel in conjunction with the second coming of Christ. The battle, or campaign, of Armageddon is described in Daniel 11:40-45; Joel 3:9-17; Zechariah 14:1-3; and Revelation 16:14-16. It will occur in the final days of the tribulation when, as John tells us, kings of the world will be gathered together "for the war of the great day of God, the Almighty" in a place known as "Har–Magedon" (Revelation 16:14,16).

The term *Armageddon* comes from the Hebrew language. *Har* is the word for "mountain," and often appears with the Hebrew definite article "H." *Mageddon* is likely the ruins of

THE BATTLE OF ARMAGEDDON

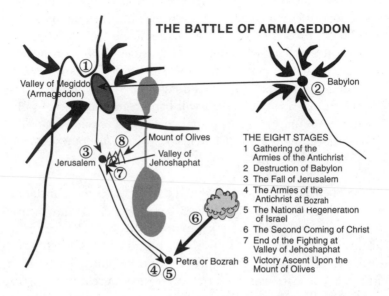

Valley of Megiddo (Armageddon)

①

Babylon ②

Jerusalem ③

Mount of Olives ⑧

Valley of Jehoshaphat

⑦

⑥

Petra or Bozrah ④⑤

THE EIGHT STAGES
1 Gathering of the Armies of the Antichrist
2 Destruction of Babylon
3 The Fall of Jerusalem
4 The Armies of the Antichrist at Bozrah
5 The National Regeneration of Israel
6 The Second Coming of Christ
7 End of the Fighting at Valley of Jehoshaphat
8 Victory Ascent Upon the Mount of Olives

an ancient city that overlooks the Valley of Esdraelon in northern Israel. The site for the converging of the armies is the plain of Esdraelon, around the hill of Megiddo. The area is located in northern Israel about 20 miles south-southeast of Haifa.

According to the Bible, great armies from the east and the west will gather and assemble on this plain. There will be threats to the power of the Antichrist from the south, and he will also move to destroy a revived Babylon in the east before finally turning his forces toward Jerusalem to subdue and destroy it. As he and his armies move on Jerusalem, God will intervene and Jesus Christ will return to rescue His chosen people, Israel. The Lord and His angelic army will destroy the armies, capture the Antichrist and the False Prophet, and cast them into the lake of fire (Revelation 19:11-21).

In a sense, Armageddon is a battle that never really takes place. That is, it does not take place in accordance with its original human intent. Its human purpose is to gather the armies of the world to execute the Antichrist's "final solution" to the "Jewish problem." This is why Jesus Christ chooses this moment in history for His return to earth—to thwart the Antichrist's attempted annihilation of the Jews and to destroy the armies of the world who have been gathered. It seems only fitting, in light of mankind's bloody legacy, that the return of Christ should be precipitated by worldwide military conflict against Israel. And so it is that history is moving toward Armageddon.

Ashen (Pale) Horse Judgment
See "Four Horsemen."

B

Babylon

Scripture presents Jerusalem as God's city and Babylon as Satan's city. This "tale of two cities" is seen from Genesis to Revelation. Throughout the Bible, Babylon is prophetically important as that which birthed and continues to nurture everything associated with the kingdom of man. Set in contrast to the natural beauty of Jerusalem and her hill country setting, Babylon was founded upon the plain of Shinar. There the people built the counterfeit tower which is the expression of a rebellious human heart (tower of Babel, Genesis 11:1-9). No wonder the pseudo-program of Satan in all of its aspects—religious, social, political, and economical—finds its earthly nativity and climax in identity with Babylon.

Daniel's prophecy depicts Babylon as the fountainhead of the Gentile kingdoms that will dominate during the "times of the Gentiles," which began in 586 B.C. (when Israel fell to Nebuchadnezzar) and will not end until the second coming of Christ (Daniel 2; 7). Babylon was the most important city in the world for about 2,000 years, and the Bible tells us that it will be revived and brought onto the end-time stage to play a leading role (Revelation 14:8; 16:19; 17–18).

Jerusalem and Babylon will both be beehives of end-times activity. End-times prophecy demands that Babylon be rebuilt and become an important city in world affairs during the tribulation. Isaiah 13:19 says, "And Babylon, the beauty of kingdoms, the glory of the Chaldeans' pride, will be as when God overthrew Sodom and Gomorrah." The context of Isaiah 13 is "the day of the Lord," the most common Old Testament term for our more widely known term *tribulation*. Further, Babylon has indeed been conquered in the past, but never has she been destroyed cataclysmically (that is, "as when God overthrew Sodom and Gomorrah"). Revelation 18:16,19 echoes such a sudden destruction from the hand of God, "Woe, woe, the great city . . . for in one hour she has been laid waste!" Babylon has a great future role in history but will be utterly destroyed in a moment in the future.

Babylon is pictured in Revelation 17–18 as the source of ungodly religion, government, and economics. Virtually all unrighteous, end-time aspects of society are derived from a Babylonian source. The true character of Babylon is revealed to John in Revelation 17:5 as a mystery that is exposed as:

BABYLON THE GREAT,
THE MOTHER OF HARLOTS
AND OF THE
ABOMINATIONS OF THE EARTH

As the mother of all false religion, Babylon is the source from which arises false Christianity in our own day and certainly during the tribulation. All the streams of apostate Christianity—will converge into ecclesiastical Babylon during the tribulation (Revelation 17). These groups will continue their deceptive roles but will also experience God's judgment during and at the end of the tribulation. The same destiny is noted in Revelation 18 for commercial Babylon.

Babylon will be the focus of God's displeasure and must be judged and removed before Christ can establish His everlasting kingdom on earth. This He will accomplish through the many judgments that will occur in their own order during the tribulation. At Babylon's predestined destruction true believers will "Rejoice over her, O heaven, and you saints and apostles and prophets, because God has pronounced judgment for you against her" (Revelation 18:20).

B

Beast

Beast is the most common biblical name for the one commonly known as the Antichrist. Revelation calls him the beast 37 times in 29 verses. The reference is first applied to Antichrist in Daniel 7, where the four successive forms of the kingdom of man during the times of the Gentiles are pictured as beasts:

- *Babylon* like a lion (Daniel 7:4)
- *Medo-Persia* like a bear (Daniel 7:5)
- *Greece* like a leopard (Daniel 7:6)
- *Rome* like a ten-horned beast (Daniel 7:7ff.)

The final Roman beast is presented in its two phases: 1) the form in existence at Christ's first coming, and 2) the revived form that will be in existence as its "ten-nation federation" during the tribulation. Since the true natures of these consecutive kingdoms are disclosed from God's divine perspective, they are characterized as beasts. Note the following composition:

Fallen Humanity

+ Satanic Influence

Beastly/Animal Behavior

The Antichrist, the head of a beastly empire, is named simply "the beast."

See also "Antichrist."

Beast, Out of the Earth

Revelation 13:11 speaks of "another beast coming up out of the earth" as the False Prophet (see also Revelation 16:13;

19:20; 20:10). This beast is part of the satanic trinity that is active during the tribulation. A beast that came out of the sea (the Antichrist, Revelation 13:1) would be considered a greater mystery and therefore more dangerous than the more familiar beast coming out of the earth. So the beast out of the earth is a reference to the False Prophet, who plays a religiously oriented supporting role to the Antichrist.

Beast, Out of the Sea

Revelation 13:1 speaks of a mysterious "beast coming up out of the sea" (see Daniel 7:3; Revelation 17:15). This beast is the infamous Antichrist. Revelation 17:15 defines the sea or waters as a symbol for ". . . peoples and multitudes and nations and tongues." This means that the Antichrist will arise from out of the Gentile masses of humanity.

Beasts, Four

The four beasts of Daniel 7 are a reference to beastly description, paralleling the four metals of the statue in Daniel 2—the four stages of the kingdom of man that will dominate history until the arrival of the messianic kingdom or the millennium (Daniel 7:3,17). The four beasts are:

- *Babylon* like a lion (Daniel 7:4)
- *Medo-Persia* like a bear (Daniel 7:5)
- *Greece* like a leopard (Daniel 7:6)
- *Rome* like a ten-horned beast (Daniel 7:7ff.)

They are said to arise out of the great sea (the Mediterranean), which represents the Gentile masses of humanity who are easily whipped up by satanic winds. Daniel 7:17 says that they not only represent their respective empires but also refer to "four kings who will arise from the earth." The Antichrist, and his kingdom, is included in the final empire.

Bema

Bema is the transliteration of a Greek word used in the New Testament as a technical term to distinguish the event of rewards for believers from the final judgment of unbelievers, known as the great white throne judgment (Revelation 20:11-15). In the Roman world of New Testament times, there was a raised platform in the city square or at the coliseums where a dignitary would sit to hear civil matters or hand out rewards, usually a wreath, for competitive accomplishment. These were called a *bema*.

Paul wrote to the Corinthian believers, "For we must all appear before the judgment seat [*bema*] of Christ, that each one may be recompensed for his deeds in the body, according to what he has done, whether good or bad" (2 Corinthians 5:10). In Romans, Paul notes that "we shall all stand before the judgment seat [*bema*] of God" (Romans 14:10). First Corinthians 3:11-16; 4:1-5; 9:24-27 provide extensive discussions on the basis by which believers will be evaluated at the bema.

At the rapture, the church will be removed from the earth and be present with Christ (John 14:1-3) throughout the tribulation (Revelation 19:1-10). The bema judgment will take place in heaven while the tribulation is taking place on earth, so that the church may be adorned as Christ's bride in order to descend with Him at the second coming. That the bema evaluation of the entire church takes place after the rapture but before the second coming is seen in the fact that Revelation 19:7,8 notes that "His bride has made herself ready. And it was given to her to clothe herself in fine linen, bright and clean; for the fine linen is the righteous acts of the saints." Since the conclusion of the judgment is pictured as clothing of fine linen, the entire church must have gone through her evaluation or bema judgment by the time of the second coming.

Binding of Satan

Revelation 20:2,3 teaches that Satan will be bound during the thousand-year reign of Christ upon earth and that after the millennium he will be released for a short time. Even though some people teach that Satan is currently bound, this does not make sense since it clearly occurs *after* the second coming and *before* the millennium.

The binding of Satan should be seen in contrast with the posttribulational judgment of the Antichrist and False Prophet, who are thrown into their eternal abode, the lake of fire (Revelation 19:20). Satan's posttribulational judgment differs from his colleagues because he is not yet finished in history. After the thousand years he will be released for a little while to lead a final rebellion that is quickly crushed by God (Revelation 20:7-9). It is when he is finally finished in history—at the end of the millennium—that he is thrown with all the other rebels of history into the lake of fire.

Satan must be bound during the millennium because God is demonstrating during that period that even with every external source of temptation removed mankind is still in rebellion against God and in need of the grace of God. Satan is released at the end of the millennium to draw out for final judgment those who, in the course of Christ's reign, have been secret rebels.

Birth Pangs

"Birth pangs" is used by Jesus in Matthew 24:8 (the "Olivet Discourse") to describe to His disciples some of the beginning events of the first half of the tribulation. Jesus was making an analogy between the labor leading to the birth of a child and the events of the seven-year tribulation that will lead to the second coming of Christ. According to Matthew 24:8, the birth pangs would signal the beginning of the tribulation—not the second coming.

Jeremiah 30:5-7 uses the same imagery of childbirth, intense suffering, and expectation:

> For thus says the Lord, "I have heard a sound of terror, of dread, and there is no peace. Ask now, and see, if a male can give birth. Why do I see every man with his hands on his loins, as a woman in childbirth? And why have all faces turned pale? Alas! for that day is great, there is none like it; and it is the time of Jacob's distress, but he will be saved from it."

Christ undoubtedly had Jeremiah in mind when making His statement in the Olivet Discourse to birth pangs since both are spoken within the context of the tribulation. Rabbinical Judaism developed its doctrine of the tribulation around the phrase "birth pangs of the Messiah." This rabbinical understanding must have also arisen from their study of Jeremiah as well and would likely provide another reason why our Lord used the expression.

As a woman must suffer through the pain of labor in order to experience the joy of bringing a new child into the world, so Israel must suffer through the progressively intense trials of the tribulation before realizing the joys of the birth of the messianic kingdom.

Black Horse Judgment
See "Four Horsemen."

Blessed Hope

The "blessed hope" is a New Testament expression found in Titus 2:13 that is understood to refer to the rapture by pre-tribulationists and the second coming by other traditions. Paul says, "For the grace of God has appeared . . . [instructing us] to live sensibly, righteously and godly in the present age, looking for the blessed hope and the appearing of the glory of our great God and Savior, Christ Jesus" (Titus 2:11-13).

Throughout the New Testament, the coming of the Lord is presented as our hope for the future (see, for example, Romans 5:2; 8:20-25; 12:12; 15:4; 2 Corinthians 1:10; 3:12; Galatians 5:5; Colossians 1:15,27; 1 Thessalonians 1:3; 2:19; 4:13). It is described as a hope because that is when believers will receive their sinless, resurrection bodies, which is also known in the New Testament as a time or hope of glory. This hope of glory is often called by the theological term "glorification." Thus, at this especially tender moment in his letter to Titus, Paul speaks of the time of glory as a *blessed* hope.

Bodies, Glorified and Resurrected

The Bible teaches that the bodies we will have in heaven will be our own earthly bodies—but resurrected and glorified. They will have the same qualities as the glorified resurrection body of Jesus Christ. Paul notes in Philippians 3:21 that Jesus Christ "will transform the body of our humble state into conformity with the body of His glory, by the exertion of the power that He has even to subject all things to Himself." Believers will have a body for eternity, but the next one we receive will be different in some aspects than our current model.

The church-age believer will be glorified and resurrected at the rapture (1 Corinthians 15:51-58; 1 Thessalonians 4:13-18).

Those believers who are alive when the rapture occurs will be translated immediately without having to experience death. For believers from different eras of history, it will take place at different times. For example, Old Testament saints will be resurrected at the second coming (Daniel 12:1), while millennial believers will be resurrected at the end of that period of time.

In our resurrection bodies the effects of the fall and of sin will be removed. The bodies will be real but without the physical limitations we presently experience and without the effects of disease, disability, or tragedy. We will have recognizable spiritual bodies just like Jesus Christ had after His resurrection. The apostle John writes in 1 John 3:2, "We know that, when He appears, we shall be like Him, because we shall see Him just as He is."

Bones, Dry

Ezekiel 37 records an extraordinary prophetic event known as the "valley of dry bones." In his vision, Ezekiel describes an end-time reconstitution of the nation of Israel in terms of a reversal of the death and decay of a body. The prophecy pictures a valley of dry, dusty bones apparently congregated as the residue of a battle in the distant past. Then suddenly life starts flowing into the bones and the reconstitution begins. A very clear four-staged process is stated in verse 6:

- put *sinews* on you
- make *flesh* grow back on you
- cover you with *skin*
- put *breath* in you

This process describes the end-time regathering and regeneration of Israel that began in 1948, when Israel became a nation. The result will be their national conversion at the end of the tribulation in preparation for the millennial reign with Jesus, their newfound Messiah. This is portrayed as a miraculous event because it is just that. No nation in history has ever been brought back from the dead as has God's elect nation, Israel.

While this passage may picture something similar to the new birth of an individual as mentioned in John 3 (when Jesus said to Nicodemus, "unless one is born again . . ."), this is not what is being prophesied when taken in context. This is a prophecy about national Israel as supported by Ezekiel 37:11: "Son of man, these bones are the whole house of Israel."

Book of Life

The book of life is the record that is opened at the great white throne judgment (Revelation 20:11,12). The book of life in the Bible refers to those who are on God's list as believers in the Lord Jesus Christ. Those who are not Christians do not have their names written in the book.

The book of life is mentioned eight times (Psalm 69:28; Philippians 4:3; Revelation 3:5; 13:8; 17:8; 20:12,15; 21:27). The imagery of the book of life in the New Testament is based on Old Testament references such as Exodus 32:32 and Psalm 69:28, which speak of God's book in which were written the names of the righteous. It was common in ancient times for a ruler to record the names of those under his domain. The book appears to be a list of the elect since Scripture says that the names were "written from the foundation of the world" (Revelation 13:8; 17:8), meaning that their salvation is sure. At the great white throne judgment, great care is taken to ensure that no one whose name is found in the book of life is cast into the lake of fire. Instead, only those whose names are not found in the book of life and who are judged according to their own works—not the work of Christ—are cast forever into the lake of fire (Revelation 20:11-15).

Bottomless Pit

Bottomless pit (or *abyss*) is the English translation of the Greek word *abussos* which literally means "boundless," or "bottomless." Seven of the nine times it appears in the Greek New Testament are in Revelation (9:1,2,11; 11:7; 17:8; 20:1,3). The bottomless pit is always seen as a holding place for beings whose ultimate, eternal abode will be the lake of fire (Revelation 20:14,15). The abyss functions like a county jail (temporary holding place) does for a prisoner. When convicted of a crime the prisoner is moved from the county jail to the state or federal penitentiary (final destiny). Beings who are being held but have future roles in history are said to be placed in the abyss. When their roles are completed, they are placed in the lake of fire. In Revelation 9 demonic locusts are released from the bottomless pit around the middle of the tribulation to torment humanity for five months. After the second coming of Christ, an angel places Satan into the abyss (Revelation 20:1-3), where he stays until he is released at the end of the millennium in order to lead his brief rebellion that God will bring to a swift end.

Bowl Judgments

The third of three series of seven judgments that take place during the tribulation is known as "bowl judgments" (Revelation 16). These judgments, when compared to the seal and trumpet judgments, appear to be the most intense and severe. It appears that these bowls have been collecting God's wrath, so to speak, for a long time. Now they are filled to the brim and ready to be poured, which will prepare the way for Christ's ascent at the second coming. The angels who administer these judgments are pictured as turning the bowls upside down to ensure that every last drop of God's wrath goes forth (see Revelation 15–16). Nothing is held back. Each judgment is specifically directed at an object of God's wrath:

- *First Bowl* (Revelation 16:1,2)—This bowl judgment is poured "into the earth" and aimed specifically at those who have taken the mark of the beast. In some measure, it is a fulfillment of Revelation 14:9-11. The judgment is an affliction of grievous, malignant sores upon the human body.
- *Second Bowl* (Revelation 16:3)—The next bowl judgment is poured "into the sea," turning the water to blood so that every living thing that was left alive from previous judgments will be killed. The stench and disease that will result from this event is unimaginable.
- *Third Bowl* (Revelation 16:4-7)—The third bowl judgment is poured "into the rivers and the springs of waters" so that all remaining fresh water is also turned to blood. The third bowl judgment is God's answer to the martyrs' prayer to be avenged (Revelation 6:10). This "water-to-blood" judgment is accompanied by two declarations from the administering angel: First, this act is in retaliation for "the blood of saints and prophets" who had died from persecution for standing for the truth. Second, the righteousness of God is revealed in this act and in all His judgments.
- *Fourth Bowl* (Revelation 16:8,9)—This judgment is poured "upon the sun" so that an extraordinary heat goes forth and scorches people with fire. In the third

B

bowl judgment the evaluation of heaven is that God is righteous and just to act this way. In this judgment the response of man on earth is reported—and it is the opposite of heaven: "They blasphemed the name of God . . . and they did not repent, so as to give Him glory."

- *Fifth Bowl* (Revelation 16:10,11)—The next bowl judgment is poured out "upon the throne of the beast" so that his whole domain is darkened with a blackout. This is similar to the darkness experienced in Egypt during the ten plagues (Exodus 10:21-23). Apparently this is not a normal darkness but is accompanied with some kind of agony that will cause people to gnaw their tongues because of the pain. Once again the response is to blaspheme "the God of heaven because of their pains and their sores; and they did not repent of their deeds."

- *Sixth Bowl* (Revelation 16:12-15)—The sixth bowl judgment is poured out "upon the great river, the Euphrates" so that its flow of water dries up. This is to prepare the way for the kings of the east to come to the mountains of Israel for the battle of Armageddon. God is clearly baiting the Antichrist and drawing him into His trap, which was set for further and final judgment at the second coming. The absolute demonic character of the satanic trinity is revealed in this judgment. Scripture notes that they will use "signs" to entice the kings of the earth to gather for Armageddon. Joel 3:9-11 and Psalm 2 are parallel passages depicting the gathering of the world's armies for Armageddon.

- *Seventh Bowl* (Revelation 16:17-21)—The last bowl judgment is poured out "upon the air" so that "flashes of lightning and sounds and peals of thunder" announce the greatest earthquake in the history of the world. This judgment apparently takes place in conjunction with the

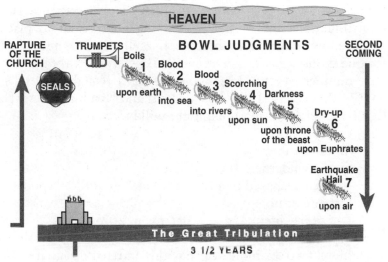

BOWL JUDGMENTS

HEAVEN

RAPTURE OF THE CHURCH

TRUMPETS

BOWL JUDGMENTS

SECOND COMING

SEALS

Boils 1

Blood 2
upon earth

Blood 3
into sea

Scorching 4
into rivers
upon sun

Darkness 5
upon throne
of the beast

Dry-up 6
upon Euphrates

Earthquake
Hail 7
upon air

666

The Great Tribulation

3 1/2 YEARS

ascent of Christ at the second coming and is also reported in Joel 3:14-17; Zechariah 14:4,5; and Matthew 24:29. This worldwide earthquake will cause Jerusalem to be split into three sections, preparing the way for millennial changes after the second coming. This is also the moment of Babylon's sudden destruction. Further, this global judgment is accompanied by 100-pound hailstones from heaven. Once again the response of the unbelievers of the world is to blaspheme "God because of the plague of the hail, because its plague was extremely severe."

Bozrah

Bozrah, *sheepfold* in Hebrew, is located in the mountain range of Mount Seir in the southern part of the modern state of Jordan. It will be to this location that the Jewish remnant will flee from the Antichrist in the middle of the tribulation (Matthew 24:15-21). Revelation 12:6,14 also speak of this midtribulation flight of the Jews living in Israel to "a place prepared by God, so that there she [Israel] might be nourished for one thousand two hundred and sixty days" (verse 6).

A number of Old Testament passages (Isaiah 33:13-16; 41:17-20; Micah 2:12), when gleaned and harmonized, teach that Israel's midtribulational flight will be:

1. in the mountains
2. in the wilderness
3. a place prepared in advance
4. very defensible
   (Fruchtenbaum, *Footsteps,* p. 202)

Daniel 11:40-45 indicates that three areas, designated by their ancient names of Edom, Moab, and Ammon, will escape the worldwide rule of Antichrist. This is the exact area where the Jewish remnant will be nurtured by the Lord through the second half of the tribulation. The city of Bozrah will be the sheepfold that will protect the Jewish remnant.

Jeremiah 49:13,14 indicates that at the end of the tribulation the Antichrist will find the Jews in Bozrah and send his armies to attack them. Hosea 6:1-3 teaches that the threatened Jewish remnant will plead in faith for Messiah to return. He will do this in order to protect the remnant, and this will lead to the eventual second coming to the Mount of Olives in Jerusalem. But the second coming will not occur until Messiah stops by His sheepfold to rescue His people. Most likely the exact location of Bozrah is the abandoned city of Petra.

See also "Petra."

C

Chiliasm

Chiliasm is the oldest term for Christ's 1,000-year kingdom in Revelation 20:1-7. The English word *chilias* is a transliteration of the Greek word for 1,000.

See also "Millennium."

Christ

"Christ" is not Jesus' last name in the modern sense. Christ is a common title that is properly attached to His given name. It comes into English from the Greek translation of the Hebrew word meaning "anointed one." Since the Messiah was to be *the* anointed one, the title Christ developed as that designation. To knowingly call Jesus "the Christ" is to recognize that He is the promised Messiah.

Christ is the focus of all history and prophecy. Everything revolves around what He will do in the future.

See also "Jesus Christ."

Church

What is the prophetic future of the church? In order to deal with this matter we must first understand that the church relates in two ways to the program of God. First, the true church is made up of Jews and Gentiles who genuinely know Christ as their Savior and have had their sins forgiven. Beginning on the day of Pentecost in Acts 2 and continuing to the rapture, all believers are part of Christ's body, the church.

Second, there is the realm of the professing church's influence, which we will call Christendom. Christendom consists of any and every thing associated with the visible church, including all of its branches such as Roman Catholicism, Eastern

41

Orthodox, Protestantism, and even the cults. Christendom includes true believers and mere professors, the wheat and the tares growing up together (Matthew 13:24-30). Each of these two aspects of the church have very different prophetic destinies.

The next event on the prophetic calendar for the true church is the rapture (see John 14:1-3; 1 Corinthians 15:51,52; 1 Thessalonians 4:13-18). This event is described in 1 Thessalonians 4:17, which says it will be a time in which all living and dead believers "shall be caught up . . . in the clouds to meet the Lord in the air." This event could happen at any moment without warning and fits the motif of Christ as groom and the church as bride. In the present age the church is betrothed to Christ—totally committed having been bought by His blood. The groom has gone away to the Father's house to prepare a place to which to He can bring His bride. While He is away (the current church age), the bride's faithfulness is tested by the separation. She is to remain faithful while constantly watching for His un-announced return. When the Father gives the signal, the shout will go forth and the church age will be completed at the rap-ture—when all true believers will always be with the Lord.

However, the rest of "Christendom" will be left behind to enter into the tribulation period as Satan's harlot—"the great harlot who sits on many waters" (Revelation 17:1)—who will help facilitate the great delusion of Antichrist in the form of the world church. This ecumenical and apostate church will pave the way for a one-world religion—the worship of Antichrist and reception of the mark of the beast (Revelation 13:16-18). It is significant to observe that Revelation 13:11-18 presents the False Prophet (head of the one-world church during the tribulation) as the one who is advocating, on be-half of the Antichrist, reception of the number 666. Just as the true church has its role of declaring and making clear the truth of God, so Satan's harlot has a leading role in fostering his deception.

The church is unique in the plan of God and separate from His plan for Israel. The church partakes of the spiritual promises of the Abrahamic covenant as fulfilled through Christ. Israel—not the church—will fulfill its national destiny as a separate entity, during the millennium (after the rapture and tribulation). The New Testament teaches that the church was an unrevealed mystery in the Old Testament (Romans 16:25,26; Ephesians 3:2-10; Colossians 1:25-27), which is why it began suddenly, without warning (Acts 2), and why this age will end suddenly and mysteriously at the rapture. The church has no nonresurrected, earthly prophetic destiny beyond the rapture.

The New Testament teaches that the church will be removed at the rapture before the time of the tribulation begins (1 Thessalonians 1:10; 5:9; Revelation 3:10) and taken by Christ to the Father's house (John 14:1-3). The church will be in heaven during the tribulation, as represented by the 24 elders (Revelation 4:4,9-11; 7:13,14; 19:4), and during the seven years it will undergo the bema judgment in preparation for accompanying Christ at His descent at the second coming (Revelation 19:11-14). The heavenly preparation of the church during the tribulation is also pictured as "His bride has made herself ready" (Revelation 19:7) for the marriage supper of the Lamb. This takes place at the beginning of the millennium, after the second coming.

While the next event for the true church—the body of Christ—is translation from earth to heaven at the rapture, those unbelievers left in the organized church as an institution will pass into the tribulation and form the base of an apostate super-church that the False Prophet will use to aid the worldwide rule of the Antichrist (Revelation 13; 17:1-18). Dr. John Walvoord provides a prophetic checklist relating to the church, listing events that are preparation for fulfillment and actual future fulfillment.

A Prophetic Checklist for the Church

1. The rise of world Communism made possible the worldwide spread of atheism.
2. Liberalism undermines the spiritual vitality of the church in Europe and eventually America.
3. The movement toward a super-church begins with the ecumenical movement.
4. Apostasy and open denial of biblical truth is evident in the church.
5. Moral chaos becomes more and more evident because of the complete departure from Christian morality.
6. The sweep of spiritism, the occult, and belief in demons begin to prepare the world for Satan's final hour.
7. Jerusalem becomes a center of religious controversy for Arabs and Christians, while Jews of the world plan to make the city an active center for Judaism.
8. True believers disappear from the earth to join Christ in heaven at the Rapture of the church.
9. The restraint of evil by the Holy Spirit is ended.
10. The super-church combines major religions as a tool for the False Prophet who aids the Antichrist's rise to world power.
11. The Antichrist destroys the super-church and demands worship as a deified world dictator.
12. Believers of this period suffer intense persecution and are martyred by the thousands.
13. Christ returns to earth with Christians who have been in heaven during the Tribulation and ends the rule of the nations at the Battle of Armageddon.

(*Armageddon*, pp. 219–21)

The role of the church during the millennium, at which time all members of the church will have received their resurrection bodies at the rapture, is to reign and rule with Christ (Revelation 3:21). In Matthew 19:28 Jesus told His disciples, who are members of the church, that they would join Him in the kingdom and reign over the 12 tribes of Israel. Also, in 2 Timothy 2:12, Paul writes, "If we endure, we shall also reign with Him." The primary purpose of the millennium is the restoration of Israel and Christ's rule over it, but the church (as the Bride of Christ) is not absent from millennial activities.

Scripture is not clear as to whether Israel, the church, and other believer groups will maintain their distinctions throughout eternity.

Church Age

The church age began on the day of Pentecost (Acts 2) and will end with the rapture of the church before the beginning of the tribulation. The church age is not characterized by historically verifiable prophetic events, except her beginning on the day of Pentecost and her ending with the rapture. But the general course of this age has been prophesied and a general overview of what can be expected during this time can be discerned.

There are three sets of passages in the New Testament that give us insights into the course of the church age.

Matthew 13   Matthew 13 surveys this present age in its relation to the kingdom with parables that cover the period of time between Christ's two advents—His first and second comings. This includes the tribulation, the second coming, and the final judgment (after the rapture), but it also includes an important overview of our present era. How does Matthew 13 depict this age? Dr. J. Dwight Pentecost summarizes:

We may summarize the teaching as to the course of the age by saying: (1) there will be a sowing of the Word throughout the age, which (2) will be imitated by a false counter-sowing; (3) the kingdom will assume huge outer proportions, but (4) be marked by inner doctrinal corruption; yet, the Lord will gain for Himself (5) a peculiar treasure from among Israel, and (6) from the church; (7) the age will end in judgment with the unrighteous excluded from the kingdom to be inaugurated and the righteous taken in to enjoy the blessing of Messiah's reign (*Things to Come*, p. 149).

Revelation 2–3 The next major passage providing an overview of the course of this age is found in the presentation of the seven churches of Revelation 2 and 3. The perspective of these two chapters is in reference to the program of the church, not the kingdom. Its overview proceeds from pentecost to the rapture as indicated by the often-repeated phrase, "He who has an ear, let him hear what the Spirit says to the churches" (Revelation 2:7,11,17,29; 3:6,13,22). These seven historical churches of the first century provide a pattern for the types of churches that will exist throughout church history. (For an overview of the seven churches see also "Seven Churches of Revelation.")

The Last Days for the Church The New Testament clearly speaks about the last days for the church in the epistles (New Testament letters to the churches). Interestingly, virtually all of these comments about the last days apostasy were written shortly before the death of each apostle writing (that is, during the last days of the various apostles), as if to emphasize the dangers latent during the church's last days. The following is a list of the seven major passages that deal with the last days for the church: 1 Timothy 4:1-3; 2 Timothy 3:1-5;

4:3,4; James 5:1-8; 2 Peter 2; 3:3-7; the book of Jude. Every one of these passages emphasizes over and over again that the great characteristic of the final time of the church will be that of *apostasy*. Dr. Pentecost concludes:

> This condition at the close of the age is seen to coincide with the state within the Laodicean Church, before which Christ must stand to seek admission. In view of its close it is not surprising that the age is called an "evil age" in Scripture (*Things to Come*, p. 155).

The New Testament pictures the condition within the professing church at the end of the age by a system of denials.

- Denial of *God*—Luke 17:26; 2 Timothy 3:4,5
- Denial of *Christ*—1 John 2:18; 4:3; 2 Peter 2:6
- Denial of *Christ's return*—2 Peter 3:3,4
- Denial of *the faith*—1 Timothy 4:1,2; Jude 3,4
- Denial of *sound doctrine*—2 Timothy 4:3,4
- Denial of *the separated life*—2 Timothy 3:1-7
- Denial of *Christian liberty*—1 Timothy 4:3,4
- Denial of *morals*—2 Timothy 3:1-8,13; Jude 18
- Denial of *authority*—2 Timothy 3:4

(Pentecost, *Things to Come*, p. 155)

Dr. Lewis Sperry Chafer, founder and first president of Dallas Theological Seminary, characterized the last days for the church:

> A very extensive body of Scripture bears on the last days for the Church. Reference is to a restricted time at the very end of, and yet wholly within, the present age. Though this brief period immediately precedes the great tribulation and in some measure is a preparation for it, these two times of apostasy

and confusion—though incomparable in history—are wholly separate the one from the other. Those Scriptures which set forth the last days for the Church give no consideration to political or world conditions but are confined to the Church itself. These Scriptures picture men as departing from the faith (1 Timothy 4:1-2). There will be a manifestation of characteristics which belong to unregenerate men, though it is under the profession of "a form of godliness" (cf. 2 Timothy 3:1-5). The indication is that, having denied the power of the blood of Christ (cf. 2 Timothy 3:5 with Romans 1:16; 1 Corinthians 1:23-24; 2 Timothy 4:2-4), the leaders in these forms of righteousness will be unregenerate men from whom nothing more spiritual than this could proceed (cf. 1 Corinthians 2:14) (*Systematic Theology,* vol. IV, p. 375).

The clear course of the last days for the church consists of constant warnings to the believer to be on guard against doctrinal defection (apostasy). Such a characteristic provides a clear sign of the end times for the Christian today.

These passages paint a general picture of the course of this age. All three indicate that apostasy will characterize Christendom during the time leading up to the rapture.

Even specific prophecy that is fulfilled during the church age relates to God's prophetic plan for Israel and not directly to the church. For example, the prophesied destruction of Jerusalem and her temple in A.D. 70 relates to Israel (Matthew 23:38; Luke 19:43,44; 21:20-24). It is not inconsistent that prophetic preparations relating to Israel are already underway with the reestablishment of Israel as a nation in 1948, even though we still are living in the church age.

Clouds
Clouds often accompany visible appearances of God throughout Scripture and are mentioned often in many biblical

passages of future prophetic events. The Bible speaks of two kinds of clouds: 1) natural clouds that often produce rain, and 2) the cloud of God's glory that often accompanies Him when He reveals Himself visibly to humanity. The second type of cloud was called "Shechinah glory" by the Jewish rabbis. The Shechinah glory is the visible manifestation of the presence of God, often said to be in the form of a cloud, but it could also present itself in the form of light, fire, or combinations of these.

Cloud appearances relating to prophecy include the rapture of believers who will meet Christ "in the clouds" (1 Thessalonians 4:17), and Christ's second coming which will "see the Son of Man coming on the clouds of the sky with power and great glory [that is, Shechinah glory]" (Matthew 24:30). At Christ's ascension into heaven after His resurrection, Acts 1:9 tells us that "He was lifted up while they were looking on, and a cloud received Him out of their sight." This cloud was undoubtedly a manifestation of the Shechinah glory, the Lord's trademark throughout history. This provides the basis for the two angels to declare to the onlookers that Christ will return on a cloud: "This Jesus, who has been taken up from you into heaven, will come in just the same way as you have watched Him go into heaven" (Acts 1:11). Daniel saw in a vision that Messiah would come "with the clouds of heaven" when He sets up His kingdom (Daniel 7:13).

See also "Shechinah Glory."

Covenants

God's relationship with man is always mediated through one or more of the biblical covenants. God has contracted to perform certain things in history, and prophecy concerns itself with how and when these promises will ultimately be fulfilled.

What is the nature of the biblical covenants? First, covenants are contracts between individuals for the purpose of governing that relationship. God wants to bind Himself to His people—to keep His promises so that He can demonstrate in history what kind of God He is. Second, relationships in the Bible—especially between God and man—are legal or judicial. This is why they are mediated through covenants. Covenants usually involve intent, promises, and sanctions. There are three kind of covenants in the Bible:

- The *Royal Grant* treaty (unconditional)—a promissory covenant that arose out of a king's desire to reward a loyal servant. Examples:
  —Abrahamic covenant
  —Davidic covenant

- *Suzerain-Vassal* treaty (conditional)—bound an inferior vassal to a superior suzerain and was binding only on the one who swore. Examples:
  —Chedorlaomer (Genesis 14)
  —Jabesh-gilead serving Nahash (1 Samuel 11:1)
  —Adamic covenant
  —Noahic covenant
  —Mosaic covenant (Deuteronomy)

Suzerain-Vassal Treaty Format of Deuteronomy
  —Preamble (1:1-5)
  —Historical prologue (1:6–4:49)
  —Main provisions (5:1–26:19)
  —Blessing and curses (27:1–30:20)
  —Covenant continuity (31:1–33:29)

Suzerain-Vassal treaties or covenants are unconditional. This point is important for Bible prophecy because at stake is whether or not God is obligated to fulfill His promise specifically to the original parties of the covenant. For example, we believe that God must fulfill to Israel as a national entity those promises made to them through unconditional covenants like the Abrahamic, Davidic, and Palestinian. If this is true, then they must be fulfilled literally—and that means many aspects are yet to come. Dr. Arnold Fruchtenbaum has said:

> An unconditional covenant can be defined as a sovereign act of God whereby God unconditionally obligates Himself to bring to pass definite promises, blessings, and conditions for the covenanted people. It is a unilateral covenant. This type of covenant is characterized by the formula "I will," which declares God's determination to do exactly as He promised. The blessings are secured by the grace of God (*Israelology,* p. 570).

- The *Parity* treaty—bound two equal parties in a relationship and provided conditions as stipulated by the participants. Examples:
  —Abraham and Abimelech (Genesis 21:25-32)
  —Jacob and Laban (Genesis 31:43-50)
  —David and Jonathan (1 Samuel 18:1-4; see also 2 Samuel 9:1-13)
  —Christ and church-age believers, that is, "friends" (John 15)

There are at least eight covenants in the Bible:

- The *Edenic* covenant (Genesis 1:28-30; 2:15-17)
- The *Adamic* covenant (Genesis 3:14-19)
- The *Noahic* covenant (Genesis 8:20–9:17)
- The *Abrahamic* covenant (for example, Genesis 12:1-3)
- The *Mosaic* covenant (Exodus 20–23; Deuteronomy)

51

- The *Davidic* covenant (2 Samuel 7:4-17)
- The *Palestinian* covenant (Deuteronomy 30:1-10)
- The *New* covenant (for example, Jeremiah 31:31-37)

Central to the study of Bible prophecy is how the covenants relate to Israel. The following chart illustrates their outworking and applications.

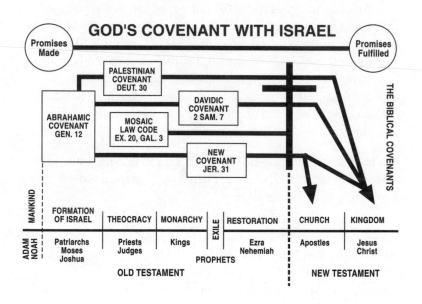

Covenant Theology

Covenant theology is not a system of theology developed from the biblical covenants, as one might first suspect. Instead, it is a system of theology based on two abstract covenants in an attempt to organize Scripture. The following is a statement of covenant theology by one proponent:

It represents the whole of Scripture as being covered by two covenants: (1) the covenant of works, and (2) the covenant of grace. The *parties* to the former covenant were God and Adam. The promise of the covenant was life. The proviso was perfect obedience by Adam. And the penalty of failure was death. To save man from the penalty of his disobedience, a second covenant, made for all eternity, came into operation, namely, the covenant of grace. . . .

The covenant of grace is treated under two aspects. The first is a Godward aspect, under which it is sometimes called the covenant of redemption. The *parties*, under this aspect, are God and Christ; the *proviso* is the Son's perfect obedience even to his suffering the penalty of man's disobedience, namely, death; and the *promise* is the salvation of all believers, *parties* are God and the believer; the *promise* eternal life; and the *proviso* faith in Jesus Christ as the only "work" required of the believer (John 6:29) (E. Harrison, *Baker's Dictionary of Theology,* p. 144).

Covenant theology has many wonderful aspects to it, such as its emphasis on the grace of God; however, it is not the product of an inductive study of the Bible. This approach does not allow for God's single decree or plan to be worked out in history through multiple programs like Israel and the church. It reduces God's multifaceted plan to a single people—the saved of eternity. Covenant theology is often hostile to a literal and futurist understanding of prophecy.

Crowns

A special subclass of rewards are called "crowns" in the New Testament. The Greek word for crown is *stephanos*, which means "that which surrounds" or "encompasses." Specifically it referred to a wreath or garland (as opposed to a crown worn by a king) and was given as a prize for victory in games and other competitive events in the ancient world. The New Testament teaches that there will be five crowns given to certain church-age believers, presumably at the judgment seat of Christ. Those five crowns are:

- Crown of righteousness—for "all who have loved His appearing" (2 Timothy 4:8).
- Incorruptible crown—for each person who "exercises self-control in all things" (1 Corinthians 9:24-27).
- Crown of glory—for faithful pastors of local congregations who "will receive the unfading crown of glory" (1 Peter 5:1-4).
- Crown of rejoicing—a special crown for those who have led others to faith in Christ (1 Thessalonians 2:19).
- Crown of life—for those who have endured special suffering: "He will receive the crown of life, which the Lord has promised to those who love Him" (James 1:12).

D

Daniel, Book of

Daniel and Revelation are two of the most important books of the Bible relating to future prophetic events because they provide key information about the players and time sequences of end-time prophecy. Daniel introduces many of the items that Revelation expands upon. Daniel is the fountainhead out of which springs the major themes of Bible prophecy. It is impossible to understand prophecy without knowing the book of Daniel.

The book of Daniel contains graphic prophetic visions which provide an outline of what God would do from the sixth century B.C., when Daniel lived and wrote, until the coming of Messiah's kingdom (the millennium). The key prophetic chapters are Daniel 2, 7, 9, 11, and 12. Chapters 2, 7, and 9 provide chronological outlines for Jewish and Gentile history.

God gave Daniel and the nation of Israel an outline of their history during the Babylonian captivity to give them hope—the assurance that He would work out His plan for them in the future. Daniel chapters two and seven provide an overview of four Gentile kingdoms that will dominate world history until Israel and her Messiah crush them and rules from that time on. The first of the four kingdoms was Babylon, under whose jurisdiction Daniel saw and wrote many of his prophetic vision in the sixth century B.C. The other kingdoms that will arise before Messiah's will be Medo-Persia, Greece, and Rome. The Roman Empire will undergo a revival and become a ten-nation confederacy right before the coming of Messiah's final realm. Daniel 2 records these kingdoms from a Gentile perspective, while Daniel 7 repeats the overview from God's perspective (which explains why they are characterized as beasts).

D

One of the most important passages relating to Bible prophecy is Daniel 9:24-27, in which is revealed the famous "70 weeks" for Israel's history. It is from this passage that Israel should have known when Messiah would come the first time, and it is from these verses that we know the end-time tribulation will last seven years. Daniel 9:24-27 also contains many other important prophetic elements.

Daniel 11 and 12 provide necessary information for the student of prophecy. For example, Daniel 11 gives many details relating to the Antichrist. Daniel 12 provides further chronology for the tribulation and lets us know that there will be an interval of 75 days between Christ's second coming and the beginning of the millennium.

See also "Daniel's 70 weeks."

Harmony of Daniel 2 and 7

Chapter 2 Nebuchadnezzar's Dream of the Image		History		Chapter 7 Daniel's Vision of the Four Beasts	
Prophecy		Fulfillment		Prophecy	
Dream 2:31-35	Interpretation 2:36-45	World Empires		Interpretation 7:15-28	Dream 7:1-14
1 2:32 Head (Gold)	2:38 You-- Nebuchadnezzar	Babylonian 612-539 B.C.		1 7:17 King	7:4 Lion with wings of an eagle
2 2:32 Breasts and Arms (Silver)	2:39 Inferior Kingdom	Medo-Persian 539-331 B.C.		2 7:17 King	7:5 Bear raised up on one side
3 2:32 Belly and Thighs (Bronze)	2:39 Third Kingdom	Grecian 331-63 B.C.		3 7:17 King	7:6 Leopard with four heads and four wings on its back
4 2:33 Legs (Iron) Feet (Iron & Clay)	2:40 Fourth Kingdom	Rome	Ancient Rome 63 B.C.-A.D. 476	4 7:23 Fourth Kingdom	7:7,19 Fourth beast with iron teeth and claws of bronze
			Revived Roman Empire	7:24 Ten Kings	7:7,8 Ten horns
				7:24 Different King	7:8 Little horn uttering great boasts
2:35 Great Mountain	2:44 Kingdom which will never be destroyed	Messianic Kingdom		7:27 Everlasting Kingdom	7:9 Thrones were set up

Daniel, Four Kingdoms of

A central theme in the prophetic visions of Daniel is the depiction of the four Gentile kingdoms that play an important role in history. These four kingdoms are introduced through Nebuchadnezzar's dream in Daniel 2 and repeated in the form of four beasts in Daniel 7. These four kingdoms make up the kingdom of man that is set in opposition to God's kingdom. The fourth kingdom will play a significant role in end-time prophecy.

The four kingdoms are first revealed in Daniel 2:29-35, which describes a large statue of a man whose body parts were made of different metals. The head was of pure gold, the chest area and arms were of silver, the hips and thighs were made of bronze, the legs were made of iron, and the feet were composed of iron and baked clay.

Daniel explains the meaning of the dream in verses 36-45. He points out that history will be dominated by the rise to world power of a series of Gentile nations. These Gentile nations will rule the world until they are destroyed by a fifth and final kingdom—God's kingdom involving national Israel. In the Bible, this period of Gentile domination and the four kingdoms, which started with the rise of Babylon in 586 B.C., is called "the times of the Gentiles."

The revelation of four Gentile kingdoms is repeated in a different setting in Daniel 7. This time, instead of depicting the kingdoms as a statue, they are revealed as four beasts. The four kingdoms in Daniel 2 and 7 are:

- *Babylon* (612–539 B.C.)—represented by the head of gold and a lion having the wings of an eagle (2:32; 7:4).
- *Medo-Persia* (539–331 B.C.)—represented by the silver upper body and a bear (2:32; 7:5).

- *Greece* (331–63 B.C.)—represented by the belly and thighs made of bronze and a leopard with four wings and four heads (2:32; 7:6).
- *Rome* (63 B.C.–A.D. 476; tribulation)—represented by legs of iron and an unspecified beast with iron teeth and bronze claws (2:33; 7:7,17).

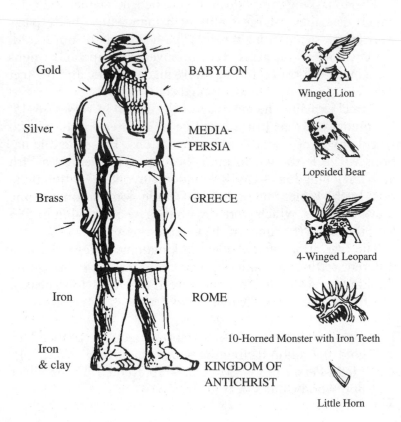

Gold — BABYLON — Winged Lion

Silver — MEDIA-PERSIA — Lopsided Bear

Brass — GREECE — 4-Winged Leopard

Iron — ROME — 10-Horned Monster with Iron Teeth

Iron & clay — KINGDOM OF ANTICHRIST — Little Horn

Since the first three kingdoms, in addition to the first phase of the fourth, are past, Daniel 7 gives some detail about the final form of the fourth kingdom often known as the "Revived Roman Empire." At this point, Daniel begins speaking about events that are related to end-time prophecy. Daniel 7:7 speaks of the rise of a ten-horned phase of the fourth kingdom that represents the Antichrist's kingdom during the tribulation (7:20-28). One of the horns is called "the little horn" (7:8). This is the Antichrist who rises up and dominates the ten-nation confederacy and eventually rules the world (7:23). Daniel records for us the role that the fourth kingdom has as the facilitator of Antichrist's kingdom during the tribulation.

The book of Revelation builds upon Daniel's revelation and further develops the final phase of the fourth kingdom that will play such a significant role during the tribulation as Antichrist's kingdom. Dr. John Walvoord notes:

> The minute description given here of the end time, the fourth beast, and the ten horns followed by the eleventh horn that gained control of three has never been fulfilled in history. Some expositors have attempted to find ten kings of the past and the eleventh king who would arise to somehow fulfill this prophecy, but there is nothing corresponding to this in the history of the Roman Empire. The ten horns do not reign one after the other, but they reign simultaneously. Further, they were not the world empire, but they were the forerunner to the little horn which after subduing three of the ten horns will go on to become a world ruler (v. 23; Revelation 13:7) (*Prophecy Knowledge Handbook,* p. 233).

The four kingdoms of Daniel play a major role in history. The final form of the fourth will be the Revived Roman

Empire, which will be reconstituted in Europe and is the focus of the Antichrist's kingdom during the tribulation. In order to have an understanding of end-time events, one must know the role these four kingdoms play.

Daniel's 70 Weeks

The "70 weeks" prophesied in Daniel 9:24-27 are the framework within which the seven-year tribulation (or the seventieth week) occurs. The prophecy of the 70 weeks was given to Daniel by God while Daniel was living under Babylonian captivity (Daniel 9:1; 2 Chronicles 36:21-23; Ezra 1; 6:3-5). Daniel was concerned for his people who were nearing the end of their 70-year captivity. In his vision he was reassured that God had not forgotten His chosen people. The angel Gabriel told Daniel that God would bring Israel back into its land and would one day set up the messianic kingdom. What was unexpected for Daniel was the revelation that all of this would not be fulfilled at the end of the current 70-year captivity in Babylon but after a future 70-week period described in 9:24-27. According to Daniel 9:27, the Antichrist will emerge in power during the prophetic milestone known as the seventieth week and after the fulfillment of the previously prophesied "69 weeks":

> And he [the Antichrist] will make a firm covenant with the many for one week, but in the middle of the week he will put a stop to sacrifice and grain offering; and on the wing of abominations will come one who makes desolate, even until a complete destruction, one that is decreed, is poured out on the one who makes desolate.

It is this seventieth week, a future seven-year period, that is the tribulation. This era follows the rapture of the church and will be a time of unparalleled suffering and turmoil. The seven-year period of Daniel's seventieth week provides the time span to which a whole host of descriptives are associated. Some of these terms are: tribulation, great tribulation, day of the Lord, day of wrath, day of distress, day of trouble, time of Jacob's trouble, day of darkness and gloom, and wrath of the Lamb.

At the beginning of the second half of the seventieth week (seventieth "seven"), the Antichrist will break the covenant he has made with Israel, and it will remain broken for three-and-a-half years. This is what is referred to as "time, times, and half a time" (Daniel 7:25; 12:7; Revelation 12:14). Since the first 69 weeks (69 "sevens") were fulfilled literally, the seventieth "seven," which is yet unfulfilled, must also be fulfilled literally.

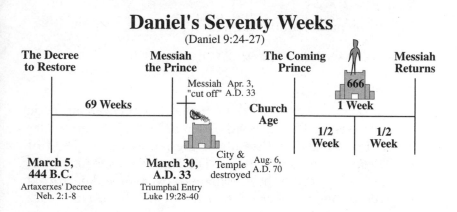

Daniel's Seventy Weeks
(Daniel 9:24-27)

The Decree to Restore	69 Weeks	Messiah the Prince	Church Age	The Coming Prince	1 Week	Messiah Returns

Messiah Apr. 3, "cut off" A.D. 33

666

1/2 Week   1/2 Week

March 5, 444 B.C.
Artaxerxes' Decree
Neh. 2:1-8

March 30, A.D. 33
Triumphal Entry
Luke 19:28-40

City & Temple destroyed
Aug. 6, A.D. 70

61

Explanation of Daniel's 70 Weeks of Years

$69 \times 7 \times 360 = 173,880$ days

March 5, 444 B.C. + 173,880 = March 30, A.D. 33

Verification

444 B.C. to A.D. 33 = 476 years

476 years × 365.2421989 days = 173,855 days

plus days between March 5 and March 30 = 25 days

Total = 173,880 days

Rationale for 360-day years

½ week—Daniel 9:27

Time, times, ½ time—Daniel 7:25; 12:7; Revelation 12:14

1,260 days—Revelation 12:6; 11:3

42 months—Revelation 11:2; 13:5

Thus: 42 months = 1,260 days = time, times,
½ time + ½ week

Therefore: month = 30 days; year = 360 days

(Hoehner, *Chronological Aspects*, p. 139)

Davidic Covenant

The Davidic covenant is an unconditional covenant made between God and King David (2 Samuel 7:4-17; 1 Chronicles 17:10-15). King David stands as the representative head of the Davidic house and dynasty. The Davidic covenant amplifies the seed aspect of the Abrahamic covenant and narrowed the seed to one member of the tribe of Judah—David. Jesus Christ is the ultimate fulfillment of many aspects of this covenant. The Davidic covenant is important to biblical prophecy because it has not yet reached its climax, but it will do so during the millennial reign of Christ.

The seven main provisions of the Davidic covenant are:

1. David is promised an eternal (indestructible) house or *dynasty* (2 Samuel 7:11b,16; 1 Chronicles 17:10b).
2. One of David's own sons, specifically *Solomon*, was to be established on the throne after David (2 Samuel 7:12).
3. Solomon, not David, would build the *temple* (2 Samuel 7:13a).
4. The *throne* of David and Solomon's kingdom was to be established forever (2 Samuel 7:13b,16). The throne emphasizes the right to rule, the authority of the king.
5. Solomon would be *disciplined* for disobedience, but God would not remove His lovingkindness from him (2 Samuel 7:14-15).

THE FOUR ETERNAL PROMISES OF THE DAVIDIC COVENANT

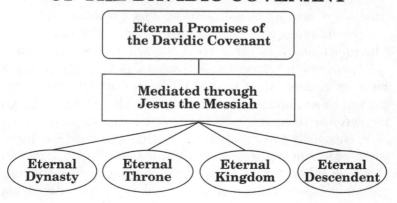

6. *Messiah* will come from the seed of David (1 Chronicles 17:11).
7. The Messiah's *throne, house,* and *kingdom* will be established forever (1 Chronicles 17:12-14).

(From Fruchtenbaum, *Israelology*, pp. 584–85)

The Davidic Covenant, since it is an unconditional and eternal covenant, is still in effect and will find its final fulfillment in future events. The covenant is also confirmed in many later biblical passages (for example, Psalm 89; Isaiah 9:6,7; 11:1; Jeremiah 23:5,6; 30:8,9; 33:14-17,19-26; Ezekiel 37:24,25; Hosea 3:4,5; Amos 9:11; Luke 1:30-35,68-70; Acts 15:14-18).

Day of the Lord
This "day" is one of the major themes of Bible prophecy. When it occurs, it involves God's direct intervention in human affairs and history. The phrase "day of the Lord" is one of numerous terms and phrases used throughout the Bible to refer to both a time of judgment (such as the tribulation) and a time of blessing (such as the millennium). In other words, the day of the Lord will literally be a day or period of time in which Jesus will impose His presence and rule, whether in judgment (the tribulation) or in glorious display (the millennium). In the current state of affairs, the Lord is not exerting His rule in a visible way. Of course, He could if He were pleased to do so, but His plan calls for the current time to be a temporary period in which He lets humanity go its own way (Romans 1:24-32).

We normally associate the day of the Lord with the future seven-year tribulation (see, for example, Zephaniah 1:14,15). However, it has a broad range of prophetic meaning. The context in which it occurs must be considered before identifying

OLD TESTAMENT TRIBULATION TERMS AND EXPRESSIONS

Tribulation Term	Old Testament Reference
1. DAY OF THE LORD	Obadiah 15; Joel 1:15; 2:1, 11,31; 3:14; Amos 5:18, 20; Isaiah 2:12; 13:6, 9; Zephaniah 1:7, 14; Ezekiel 13:5; 30:3; Zechariah 14:1
2. GREAT & TERRIBLE DAY OF THE LORD	Malachi 4:5
3. TROUBLE, TRIBULATION	Deuteronomy 4:30; Zephaniah 1:16
4. TIME/DAY OF TROUBLE	Daniel 12:1; Zephaniah 1:15
5. DAY OF JACOB'S TROUBLE	Jeremiah 30:7
6. BIRTH PANGS	Isaiah 21:3; 26:17-18; 66:7; Jeremiah 4:31; Micah 4:10 (cf. Jeremiah 30:6)
7. THE DAY OF CALAMITY	Deuteronomy 32:35; Obadiah 12-14
8. INDIGNATION	Isaiah 26:20; Daniel 11:36
9. THE [LORD'S] STRANGE WORK	Isaiah 28:21
10. OVERFLOWING SCOURGE	Isaiah 28:15, 18
11. DAY OF VENGEANCE	Isaiah 34:8a; 35:4a; 61:2b; 63:4a
12. DAY OF WRATH	Zephaniah 1:15
13. DAY OF THE LORD'S WRATH	Zephaniah 1:18
14. DAY OF DISTRESS	Zephaniah 1:15
15. DAY OF DESTRUCTION	Zephaniah 1:15
16. DAY OF DESOLATION	Zephaniah 1:15
17. DAY OF DARKNESS AND GLOOM	Zephaniah 1:15; Amos 5:18, 20; Joel 2:2
18. DAY OF CLOUDS & THICK DARKNESS	Zephaniah 1:15; Joel 2:2
19. DAY OF TRUMPET AND ALARM	Zephaniah 1:16
20. DAY OF THE LORD'S ANGER	Zephaniah 2:2, 3
21. [DAY OF] DESTRUCTION, RUIN, FROM THE ALMIGHTY	Joel 1:15
22. THE FIRE OF HIS JEALOUSY	Zephaniah 1:18

it with a specific event in God's prophetic plan. In the Old Testament the phrase was used by the prophets to refer to a coming time of judgment. In some cases that judgment is now past and in others it is yet future.

As a future time of judgment, the day of the Lord is a time of devastation and destruction (Zechariah 12:4). In the New Testament it is explicitly spoken of by Paul in 1 Thessalonians 5:2: "For you yourselves know full well that the day of the Lord will come just like a thief in the night." In this passage it refers to an extended period of time that begins just after the rapture of the church and continues through the millennium. Dr. Ryrie writes:

> Three facets of the Day of the Lord are discernible: (1) the historical, that is, God's intervention in the affairs of Israel (Zephaniah 1:14-18; Joel 1:15) and heathen nations (Isaiah 13:6; Jeremiah 46:10; Ezekiel 30:3); (2) the illustrative, whereby an historical incident represents a partial fulfillment of the eschatological Day of the Lord (Joel 2:1-11; Isaiah 13:6-13); (3) the eschatological. This eschatological "day" includes the time of the Great Tribulation (Isaiah 2:12-19; 4:1), the second coming of Christ (Joel 2:30-32), and the Millennium (Isaiah 4:2; 12; 19:23-25; Jeremiah 30:7-9) (Ryrie, *Ryrie Study Bible,* Expanded ed., p. 1392).

It is likely that when one takes into account all aspects of the future "day of the Lord," it will be a period of 1,007 years in duration. The previous chart shows most of the biblical terms used to refer to the tribulation.

Dispensationalism

Dispensationalism views the world and history as a household run by God. In this household-world, God is dispensing or administering its affairs according to His own will, in various stages of revelation in the process of time. These various stages mark off the distinguishably different economies in the outworking of God's total purpose; these economies or administrations are the dispensations. The understanding of God's differing economies is essential to a proper interpretation of His revelation within those various economies. The dispensations have nothing to do with how people are saved from their sin (that most important of issues is handled on the basis of other factors).

The dispensational view of literal interpretation supports a futurist view—that many biblical passages are meant for a future fulfillment. The distinction between Israel and the church is important because the church's present distinctiveness in the plan of God provides the theological basis for the pretribulation rapture, while Israel's Old Testament promises will be literally fulfilled in the future, which requires a detailed and sophisticated understanding of biblical prophecy.

Perhaps the leading dispensational scholar today is Dr. Charles Ryrie of Dallas Theological Seminary. He notes that *The Oxford English Dictionary* defines a theological dispensation as "a stage in a progressive revelation, expressly adopted to the needs of a particular nation or period of time. . . . Also, the age or period during which a system has prevailed." (The English word *dispensation* translates the Greek noun *oikonomía*, often rendered *administration* in modern translations. The verb *oikonoméô* refers to a manager of a household.) "In the New Testament," notes Ryrie, "*dispensation* means to manage or administer the affairs of a household, as, for example, in the Lord's story of the unfaithful steward in Luke 16:1-13" (*Dispensationalism*, pp. 25-26).

The Greek word *oikonomía* is a compound of *oikos* meaning "house" and *nomos* meaning "law." Taken together

D

"the central idea in the word *dispensation* is that of managing or administering the affairs of a household" (*Dispensationalism*, p. 25).

Ryrie continues:

The various forms of the word *dispensation* are used in the New Testament twenty times. The verb *oikoneméô* is used in Luke 16:2 where it is translated "to be a steward." The noun *oikonómos* is used ten times (Luke 12:42; 16:1,3,8; Romans 16:23; I Corinthians 4:1,2; Galatians 4:2; Titus 1:7; I Peter 4:10), and in all instances it is translated "steward" except "chamberlain" in Romans 16:23. The noun *oikonomía* is used nine times (Luke 16:2,3,4; I Corinthians 9:17; Ephesians 1:10; 3:2,9; Colossians 1:25; I Timothy 1:4). In these instances it is translated variously ("stewardship," "dispensation," "edifying"). The Authorized Version of Ephesians 3:9 has "fellowship" (*koinonia*), whereas the American Standard Version has "dispensation" (*Dispensationalism*, pp. 25–26).

Dr. Ryrie notes the following characteristics of dispensationalism:

* two parties are always involved
* specific responsibilities
* accountability as well as responsibility
* a change may be made any time unfaithfulness is found in the existing administration
* God is the one to whom men are responsible
* faithfulness is required of the subordinate party
* a stewardship may end at any time
* dispensations are connected with the mysteries of God
* dispensations and ages are connected ideas
* there are at least three dispensations (likely seven)

(*Dispensationalism*, pp. 26–27).

A *definition* of a dispensation, according to Ryrie, is "a distinguishable economy in the outworking of God's plan" (*Dispensationalism*, p. 28). A *description* of dispensationalism would include the following:

- distinctive revelation
- testing
- failure
- judgment
- a continuance of certain ordinances valid until then
- an annulment of other regulations until then valid
- a fresh introduction of new principles not before valid
- the progressive revelation of God's plan for history

(*Dispensationalism*, pp. 29–31)

Many have believed in dispensations without adhering to the system of theology known as dispensationalism. Dispensationalism combines a view of the dispensations with what Dr. Ryrie calls the three *sine qua non* (Latin, "that without which") or *essentials* of dispensationalism (*Dispensationalism*, p. 41). These are not definitions or descriptions of dispensationalism. Instead, they are basic theological tests which can be applied to an individual to see whether or not he is a dispensationalist. The three are:

- *consistent* literal interpretation
- a distinction between God's plan for Israel and the church
- the glory of God in a multifaceted way is the goal of history

We believe that the theology known today as dispensationalism can be said to at least generally represent what the Bible teaches, especially as it relates to the area of Bible prophecy. To view the Bible dispensationally is to view God's plan for history, including future prophecy, from His perspective.

Dispensations

What are the dispensations or ages in history from a biblical perspective? There are seven that can be deduced from God's Word:

- *Innocence* (Genesis 1:28–3:6)—This apparently was the shortest of the dispensations and ended in the fall into sin by the parents of the human race.
- *Conscience* (Genesis 3:7–8:14)—The title "conscience" comes from Romans 2:15 and aptly designates the time between the fall and the flood.
- *Human Government* (Genesis 8:15–11:9)—After the flood, God said He would not directly judge man until the second coming. Thus, a human agency known as civil government was divinely established to mediate and attempt to restrain the evil of man.
- *Promise* (Genesis 11:10–Exodus 18:27)—This period is dominated by the call of Abram and the promise, both physical and spiritual, made to him and his descendants.
- *Law/Israel* (Exodus 19–John 14:30)—The Israelites were never saved by keeping the law. Instead, it was how they, as a redeemed people, were to live. It was their rule of life that governed every aspect of living. But it was temporary until the coming and fulfillment by Christ.
- *Grace/Church* (Acts 2:1–Revelation 19:21)—The rule of life for the church is grace. All aspects of life are to spring forth from grace for the church-age believer. The extent of God's grace is expanded to all peoples through the worldwide offer of the gospel.
- *Kingdom* (Revelation 20:1-15)—During Messiah's 1,000-year reign from Jerusalem (upon His return to the earth), all of the promises made to Israel will be fulfilled to Israel as a nation. These promises will have been

accomplished by Christ on behalf of a now-converted Israel. The church will also reign and rule with Christ as His bride. Because Israel will be in its glory, the Gentiles will also reap great blessings as well.

Double Fulfillment

Double fulfillment means that a specific passage will be fulfilled on two or more occasions. This is not a correct approach to biblical interpretation because prophecy can only be fulfilled once. If a certain prophecy could have multiple fulfillments then it wouldn't be specific.

Sometimes Isaiah 7:14 is given as an example of double fulfillment. It is said that there was a near fulfillment in reference to a child born in Ahaz's day, but whoever that child was, it was certainly not a virgin-born baby. This is especially problematic in light of the clear statement in Matthew 1:22,23, which says specifically that Isaiah 7:14 was fulfilled in the birth of Jesus.

The Olivet Discourse (Matthew 24–25) is sometimes said to have a double fulfillment: once in the A.D. 70 destruction of Jerusalem and then again in the future tribulation in relation to the coming of Christ. This also is not possible since, in A.D. 70, the Jews were judged and killed or taken into captivity—and in the future they will be rescued and delivered from their enemies. Both cannot be true from the same passage.

Double Reference

Double reference means that in a Scripture passage part of it may be fulfilled at one time while another part may be fulfilled at another time. This is a valid law of interpretation. Double reference is something that occurs in relation to passages that speak of the career of Messiah. Looking back, we now understand that Christ's ministry would have two major phases to it. The first phase was related to His first coming and suffering and dying on the cross. Phase two is related to His second coming and is glorious and victorious. However, many passages in the Old Testament spoke of what Christ would do generally and did not distinguish whether part would be fulfilled at His first coming and another part at His return. An example of this can be found in Zechariah 9:9,10, where verse 9 was fulfilled at Christ's first advent. Verse 10 will be fulfilled at His second coming.

Dragon

In Bible prophecy "dragon" is a symbolic reference to Satan. Revelation 20:2 plainly says, "And he laid hold of the dragon, the serpent of old, who is the devil and Satan." Dragon is the favorite designation of Satan in the book of Revelation. He is called the dragon 12 other times in that book.

Revelation 12 teaches that at the midpoint of the seven-year tribulation the dragon is thrown out of heaven to the earth after a war in the heavens with Michael the archangel. Revelation 12:4 says that the dragon took one third of the stars (angels) with him in his fall. It appears that when Satan is thrown out of heaven at the midpoint of the tribulation, he enters into the Antichrist (Revelation 13:2). The three-and-a-half years that follow are the most diabolic time in all of human history, culminating in the deception and worship of the dragon through the mark of the beast.

As noted above, at the second coming the dragon is thrown into the bottomless pit for the thousand-year millennium. After that he is released for a short time to deceive unbelievers at the end of the millennium. He is then judged and cast for eternity into the lake of fire with all the other fallen angels and lost of the ages.

E

Edom

In the Old Testament, Edom covered the territory that is now southern Jordan. Jordan today is comprised of what was in biblical times Edom, Ammon, and Moab. The Edomites were the descendants of Esau, and there was continual strife between Edom and Israel. Obadiah's entire prophecy concerns Edom. In the tribulation, Edom will again be prominent as a foe of Israel. Because of Edom's intense animosity toward Israel, it will undergo total destruction in the campaign of Armageddon that will continue through the millennium (Joel 3:19; Obadiah 10).

Elijah

Elijah is related to Bible prophecy in at least two ways, one direct and the other indirect. Malachi 4:5,6 reads, "Behold, I am going to send you Elijah the prophet before the coming of the great and terrible day of the LORD. And he will restore the hearts of the fathers to their children, and the hearts of the children to their fathers, lest I come and smite the land with a curse." Such language appears to teach that Elijah will play a future role during the tribulation in the conversion of the nation of Israel by the second coming. Many believe that this return of Elijah during the tribulation will be as one of the two witnesses spoken of in Revelation 11.

Elijah pictures the rapture because he was taken directly to heaven (2 Kings 2:1,11). So it will be that a whole generation will be called home before the war of the tribulation begins, just as an ambassador is called home from a country as a sign that his country is about to engage in war.

See also "Two Witnesses."

Eschatology

A theological term from the Greek word *eschatos* meaning "last things," eschatology is the study of the last things. This term has become the primary theological expression for the study of end-time Bible prophecy. The following chart presents a summary of the future, or echatological events.

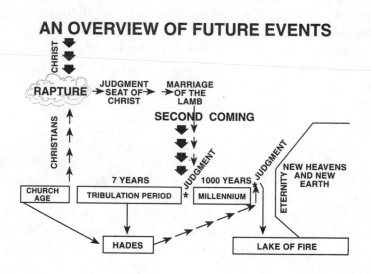

AN OVERVIEW OF FUTURE EVENTS

Eternal Life

Eternal life is the gift from God given to all who believe in Jesus Christ and have accepted His offer of salvation based upon His death and resurrection (John 10:10; Ephesians 2:8,9). In the Bible, eternal life emphasizes a quality of life— a quality that can only be imparted by God Himself. This quality does not, of course, make us God. We are and will always remain creatures; however, it is an attribute of life that comes from the God who has the quality of eternality.

Therefore, eternal life should not be confused with the endless or eternal existence that everyone will experience. Eternal existence will be common to the redeemed and the unredeemed, but the destinies will be very different (1 John 5:12). Christians will enter into heaven and the presence of God; unbelievers will be cast into the lake of fire.

Eternity

According to Revelation 21 and 22, the eternal state will begin at the end of the millennium, the thousand-year reign of Jesus Christ upon the earth. Eternity is distinct from the millennium and pertains to the perpetual destiny of all of humanity. People will either accept the free offer of salvation or reject it. Those who accept it will consciously experience everlasting life in the presence of God; those who reject it will experience everlasting conscious separation from Him. The great white throne judgment will be the transitional event between time and eternity (Revelation 20:11-15).

In relation to prophecy, we normally think of eternity as referring to the eternal state, although it also relates to the attributes of God (Hebrews 1:10-12).

Ezekiel

The prophecy of Ezekiel, penned around 592–520 B.C., was written to remind the exiles who were in Babylon of their sins, which had brought the judgment of God upon them. Ezekiel's prophecy also assured them of God's future blessing. Ezekiel was from Israel's priestly line, and he takes great interest in the temple and the priesthood in his prophecy. He gives the greatest detail concerning the millennial temple and priesthood (Ezekiel 40–48).

The first portion of the book (chapters 1–24) was written before the fall of Jerusalem and speaks of God's coming judgment on the city. The second portion of the book (chapters

25–32) speaks of prophecies and judgment against foreign nations. In the final portion of the book (chapters 33–48) the restoration of Israel and the millennial kingdom are foretold. Chapters 38–39 provide vivid descriptions of the future attack on Israel during the tribulation and the subsequent defeat of Israel's enemies. Chapters 40–48 contain detailed descriptions and prophecies of the millennial temple.

Throughout the book, God provides a message of comfort and hope. The phrase "you will know that I am the Lord" appears more than 30 times in the book. God wants His people to understand that He is justified in permitting their captivity, but He also will not forget them and will one day restore them.

F

False Prophet

The New Testament pictures three satanic persons, often called the "satanic trinity" because of their efforts to counterfeit God and His plan. These three are Satan, corresponding to God the Father; the Antichrist, juxtaposed to God the Son—Jesus Christ; and the False Prophet, who coincides with God the Holy Spirit.

The Antichrist and the False Prophet are two separate individuals who will work toward a common, deceptive goal. Their roles and relationship will be that which was common in the ancient world between a ruler (Antichrist) and the high priest (False Prophet) of the national religion (religion often facilitates political rule). The False Prophet (Revelation 16:13; 19:20; 20:10) is a prophet or spokesman for the first beast, the Antichrist. Revelation 13:11-17 states that the False Prophet, as "another beast," shares the beastly nature of the Antichrist:

> And I saw **another beast** coming up out of the earth; and he had two horns like a lamb, and he spoke as a dragon. And he exercises all the authority of the first beast in his presence. And he makes the earth and those who dwell in it to worship the first beast, whose fatal wound was healed. And he performs great signs, so that he even makes fire come down out of heaven to the earth in the presence of men. And he deceives those who dwell on the earth because of the signs which it was given him to perform in the presence of the beast, telling those who dwell on the earth to make an image to the beast who had the wound of the sword and has come to life. And there was given to him to give breath to the image of the beast, that the image of the beast might even speak and cause

as many as do not worship the image of the beast to be killed. And he causes all, the small and the great, and the rich and the poor, and the free men and the slaves, to be given a mark on their right hand, or on their forehead, and he provides that no one should be able to buy or to sell, except the one who has the mark, either the name of the beast or the number of his name (Revelation 13:11-17, emphasis added).

Dr. J. Dwight Pentecost, citing Revelation, summarizes the person and activities of the False Prophet in 11 works:

1. He is a Jew arising out of the earth, e.g., Palestine (13:11).
2. He is religiously influential (13:11).
3. He is motivated by Satan (13:11).
4. He has a delegated authority (13:12).
5. He promotes worship of the first beast (13:12).
6. He performs signs and miracles (13:13,14).
7. He deceives the unbelieving world (13:14).
8. He promotes idolatrous worship (13:14,15).
9. He has the power of death over people who do not worship the beast (13:15).
10. He has great economic power (13:16,17).
11. He will establish the mark of the beast (13:17).

(Pentecost, *Things to Come*, pp. 336–37)

The False Prophet is depicted throughout Revelation as one "who performed the signs in his [the Antichrist's] presence, by which he deceived those who had received the mark of the beast and those who worshiped his image" (Revelation 19:20). He is one who uses religion and signs and wonders to deceive the masses into worshiping the first beast, the Antichrist. Even though this is yet a future event, the lesson to be

78

learned for our own day is that one must exercise discernment, especially in the area of religion—even when miracles appear to vindicate the messenger.

Feasts of Israel

Many believe that the seven annual feasts of Israel, as given in Leviticus 23, have prophetic significance. This appears to be true, but are they fulfilled in relation to Israel or the church? The seven annual feasts are:

Spring
- Passover
- Unleavened Bread
- First Fruits
- Weeks or Pentecost

Fall
- Trumpets
- Day of Atonement
- Tabernacles

It is correctly noted that there is a prophetic aspect of Israel's feast cycle. Christ fulfilled the four feasts in the spring cycle at the exact time they was designated for celebration on Israel's annual calendar. This provides clear support for saying that the career of Christ, revolving around His two comings to earth, fulfills the seven annual feasts of Israel. Since His first coming satisfied the spring cycle, it appears certain that events related to His second coming will complete the three fall feasts. This is true, but they will be fulfilled in relation to God's plan for Israel and not in relation to God's plan for the church since the feasts relate to Israel and Israel alone. The fulfillment of Israel's feasts relates to salvation for all mankind, but the precise prophetic significance relates exclusively to national Israel.

This means that the Feast of Trumpets will be fulfilled not at the rapture of the church but at the second coming when Christ sends His angels to gather the elect from around the world and transport them to Israel for the millennium (Deuteronomy 30:4; Isaiah 11:12; Daniel 12:1; Matthew 24:31). The Day of Atonement will be fulfilled for national Israel when Messiah's atonement is applied to the nation at its conversion toward the end of the tribulation (Zechariah 12:10; Romans 11:25-27). The Feast of Tabernacles will be fulfilled for Israel during the millennium when God finally "tabernacles," or dwells, with His people.

In the New Testament, the rapture is a newly revealed event related only to the church. Therefore it could not have been predicted through Old Testament revelation such as Israel's feasts. Any use of the feasts of Israel in an attempt to date-set is invalid because it pertains to Israel, not the church.

Fig Tree

The most popular citation of the parable of the fig tree is found within Christ's sermon on prophecy, known as the Olivet Discourse, in Matthew 24:32-34:

> Now learn the parable from the fig tree: when its branch has already become tender, and puts forth its leaves, you know that summer is near; even so you too, when you see all these things, recognize that He is near, right at the door. "Truly I say to you, this generation will not pass away until all these things take place." [See Matthew 24–25; Mark 13; Luke 17:20-37; 21:5-36.]

Some people taught that this prophetic parable indicated that Christ would return within a 40-year generation of the reestablishment of Israel. The rebirth of Israel took place in 1948; therefore, Christ's coming should have occurred by 1988.

A more likely interpretation is to understand the fig tree illustration and "this generation" as a reference to those who see the events of the seven-year tribulation, especially the "abomination of desolation" (Matthew 24:15), as a sign of the second coming, not the rapture. If this interpretation is true, then it would not matter how long a generation is since the signs would not last more than seven years. Further, we can draw the same general conclusion from other biblical passages that the reestablishment of Israel constitutes a sign of the nearness of the Lord's return.

Four Horsemen

The first four seal judgments of Revelation 6:1-8 are depicted as riders on various colored horses. The first horse is white, the second red, the third black, and the fourth is ashen or pale.

White Horse Judgment   The first horse and seal judgment is the white horse (Revelation 6:2). The interpretation of this rider is hotly debated between two major views. First, that it represents Christ, and second, that it represents the Antichrist. Even though Christ does return in Revelation 19:11 on a white horse that doesn't mean that He is pictured here. The second view is more likely, since one who comes riding a white horse usually depicts a military conqueror. It is the Antichrist who comes conquering at the beginning of the tribulation, which this judgment denotes, and Christ who comes conquering the Antichrist at the end of the tribulation in Revelation 19. Some scholars believe that this judgment is parallel with Matthew 24:5.

Red Horse Judgment   The second horse and seal judgment is the red horse (Revelation 6:3,4). The red color of the horse appears to indicate blood and death since the passage says that "it was granted to take peace from the earth, and that men should slay one another; and a great sword was given to him." Some scholars believe that this judgment is parallel with Matthew 24:6,7.

Black Horse Judgment   The third horse and seal judgment is the black horse (Revelation 6:5,6). This rider comes forth displaying "a pair of scales in his hand" and saying, "A quart of wheat for a denarius, and three quarts of barley for a denarius; and do not harm the oil and the wine." A severe shortage of food is indicated. The monetary description indicates that normal purchasing power will be reduced to one-eighth. Some scholars believe that this judgment is a parallel with Matthew 24:7.

Ashen (Pale) Horse Judgment   The fourth horse and seal judgment is the ashen horse (Revelation 6:7,8). This is the most severe of the four judgments in that "over a fourth of the earth [is killed] with sword and with famine and with pestilence and by the wild beasts of the earth." Some scholars believe that this judgment is parallel with Matthew 24:7: "And in various places there will be famines and earthquakes."

Four Living Creatures

The four creatures are referred to in Revelation 4:6-8 and 19:4. Along with the 24 elders, they represent angelic and human praise. These creatures are part of God's heavenly court, having been created exclusively to worship and serve Him. They are always depicted in the act of worshiping God. The creatures are probably angels, most likely cherubim who also have multiple sets of wings, who worship God and extol His attributes (see Isaiah 6:2,3). Cherubim are a class of angels created specifically for throne-room worship and service of God.

The creatures are depicted as being like a lion, a calf, a man, and an eagle (Revelation 4:7). Tradition links these four creatures as symbols representing the four Gospels— Matthew, Mark, Luke, and John. Matthew is said to be the lion of the tribe of Judah. Mark, the servant, corresponds with the calf who served mankind as a sacrifice for sin. Luke's emphasis is on the Son of man and relates to the creature who is like a man. The flying eagle stands for John with his heavenly associations.

Fulfillment of Prophecy

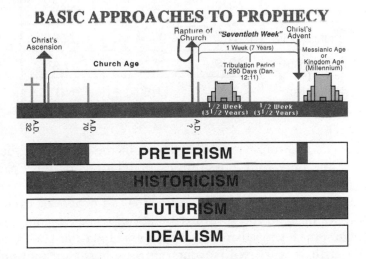

There are four possible interpretive views regarding the role of timing in Bible prophecy. The views answer the interpretive question, "When will a prophecy be fulfilled in

PROPHETIC TIMING & MILLENNIAL VIEWS

Timing	AMILL	POSTMILL	PREMILL
Preterism	YES	YES	NO
Historicism	YES	YES	YES
Futurism	NO	YES	YES
Idealism	YES	YES	NO

PREMILLENNIAL TIMING VIEWS

Timing	PRETRIB	MIDTRIB	POSTTRIB
Preterism	NO	NO	NO
Historicism	NO	YES	YES
Futurism	YES	YES	YES
Idealism	NO	NO	NO

history?" The four views are simple in the sense that they reflect the only four possibilities in relation to time: past (preterism), present (historicism), future (futurism), and timeless (idealism). Futurism states that all prophetic events will take place in the future tribulation, second coming, or millennium. Historicism says that the tribulation started in the fourth century with events surrounding Constantine's Christianization of the Roman Empire and continues until the second coming. Idealism denies that there is a timing of events. Preterism declares that the tribulation has already taken place.

The charts on page 84 show the possible interpretative blends possible in relation to millennialism and the various views of the rapture.

See also "Futurism," "Historicism," "Idealism," and "Preterism."

Fullness of Time

Ephesians 1:10 speaks of a time when all things will be summed up in Christ. This "dispensation" is called "the fullness of the times." Paul is referring to the millennial kingdom when Christ will reign over all the earth from Jerusalem. At this time, all the focus of history will be correctly upon Him, which is why this dispensation is called "the fulness of the times." All of history is moving toward this objective and will not be complete until we arrive at this future but certain goal.

Futurism

Futurism is one of four possible interpretive views regarding the role of timing in Bible prophecy. It addresses the interpretive question, "When will a prophecy be fulfilled in history?" The four views are: past (preterism), present (historicism), future (futurism), and timeless (idealism).

Futurists believe that all prophetic events will not occur in the current church age, but will take place in the future tribulation, second coming, or millennium. Of the four views noted above, the only one that logically and historically supports the pretribulational position is futurism. This is because the timing of the rapture relates to when the tribulation will occur in history. Preterism declares that the tribulation has already taken place. Historicism says that the tribulation started in the fourth century with events surrounding Constantine's Christianization of the Roman Empire and continues until the second coming. Idealism denies that there is a timing of events. Thus, futurism alone is the application of the literal method of interpretation.

A defense of futurism can be developed from the Bible by comparing and contrasting futurism with the other three approaches. For example, futurism, instead of preterism, can be shown by demonstrating from specific texts of Scripture that "coming" in the debated passages refers to a bodily return of Christ to planet Earth, not a mystical coming mediated through the Roman army. One area that supports futurism over historicism is the fact that numbers relating to days and years are to be taken literally. There is no biblical basis for days really meaning years. A major argument for futurism over idealism is the fact that numbers do count. In other words, why would God give hundreds of chronological and temporal statements in the Bible if He did not intend to indicate time?

Only the futurist can interpret the whole Bible literally and then harmonize those conclusions into a consistent theological system. Just as the people, places, and times were meant to be understood literally in Genesis 1–11, so the texts that relate to the end-times are to be taken literally. Days mean days; years mean years; months mean months. The only way that the book of Revelation and other prophetic portions of the Bible make any sense is if they are taken literally. Therefore, the end-time events have not yet happened.

The Bible is one-fourth prophecy, and a large majority of that relates to the future. Since a consistently literal approach to the Bible, including prophecy, is the best way of understanding God's revelation to man, only the futurist understanding of biblical prophecy can yield the meaning that God intended.

G

Gehenna

Gehenna, a term for eternal punishment, is used 12 times in the New Testament. *Gehenna* is derived from the Hebrew word referring to the Valley of Hinnon that runs on the south and east sides of Jerusalem. In Old Testament times the valley was a place in which pagan worshipers sacrificed infants by fire to the false god Moloch (2 Kings 16:3; 17:7,8; 21:6). Jeremiah also announced that the valley would be a place of divine judgment (Jeremiah 7:32; 19:6). The valley became a place where refuse was continually burned during New Testament times. The imagery of *Gehenna* would have been very vivid for the New Testament audience. Subsequently, the word became synonymous with eternal punishment and the fires of hell. Its usage describes the eternal punishment associated with the final judgment (Matthew 23:15,33; 25:41,46).

Gentiles

There are three major divisions of Bible prophecy: Israel, Gentiles, and the church. The Bible has much to say prophetically about the Gentiles and specific Gentile nations as they relate to both Israel and the church. In fact, it is out of a Gentile world that God calls Abram and develops the kingdom of God as set against the Gentile kingdom of man.

Revelation 17:10 speaks of "seven kings," which are the seven great Gentile powers of history. These are the worldwide empires that have always persecuted Israel:

- Egypt
- Assyria
- Babylon

G

- Medo-Persia
- Greece
- Rome
- Revived Roman Empire (Antichrist)

Dr. John Walvoord provides an extensive checklist of prophetic events relating to the Gentiles in Bible prophecy. Some of the items are setting the stage for future fulfillment during the tribulation, while others are specific prophecies to be fulfilled in history after the rapture of the church. Included in this list are:

A Prophetic Checklist for the Nations
1. The establishment of the United Nations began a serious first step toward world government.
2. The rebuilding of Europe after World War II made possible its future role in a renewal of the Roman Empire.
3. Israel was reestablished as a nation.
4. Russia rose to world power and becomes the ally of the Arab countries.
5. The Common Market and World Bank show a need for some international regulation of the world economy.
6. The Middle East becomes the most significant trouble spot in the world.
7. The oil blackmail awakens the world to the new concentration of wealth and power in the Mediterranean.
8. The Iron Curtain falls and a new order emerges in Europe.
9. Russia declines as a world power and loses her influence in the Middle East.

10. A world clamor for peace follows the continued disruption caused by the high price of oil, terrorist incidents, and the confused military situation in the Middle East.

11. Ten nations create a united Mediterranean Confederacy—beginnings of the last stage of the prophetic fourth world empire.

12. In a dramatic power play, a new Mediterranean leader upsets three nations of the confederacy and takes control of the powerful ten-nation group.

13. The new Mediterranean leader negotiates a "final" peace settlement in the Middle East (broken three-and-a-half years later).

14. The Russian army attempts an invasion of Israel and is miraculously destroyed.

15. The Mediterranean leader proclaims himself world dictator, breaks his peace settlement with Israel, and declares himself to be God.

16. The new world dictator desecrates the temple in Jerusalem.

17. The terrible judgments of the Great Tribulation are poured out on the nations of the world.

18. Worldwide rebellion threatens the world dictator's rule as armies from throughout the world converge on the Middle East.

19. Christ returns to earth with His armies from heaven.

20. The armies of the world unite to resist Christ's coming and are destroyed in the Battle of Armageddon.

21. Christ establishes His millennial reign on earth, ending the times of the Gentiles.

(Armageddon, pp. 222–23)

During Messiah's kingdom, which we know as the millennium, the Gentiles will play a significant role. Israel will be the head nation during this time (Isaiah 14:1,2), but Messiah will deal justly with the Gentiles (Isaiah 49:5-7). The Gentiles will have an obligation to observe the Feast of Tabernacles (or Booths), and if a given nation does not observe this feast God will send plagues upon them (Zechariah 14:16-19). Paul calls this time for both Jews and Gentiles an even greater fullness in Christ than saved Jews and Gentiles are currently experiencing in the church (Romans 11:12).

The role of various Gentile nations during the millennium is mentioned specifically in a number of biblical passages. Nations such as Lebanon (Ezekiel 47:13–48:29), Jordan (Jeremiah 49:7-13; Ezekiel 35:6-9), Egypt (Isaiah 19:16-22; Ezekiel 29:1-16; Joel 3:19), Assyria (which composes part of modern Iraq and Syria) (Isaiah 19:23-25), Kedar and Hazor or Saudi Arabia (Jeremiah 49:28-33), Elam or parts of Iran (Jeremiah 49:34-39). Babylon and Edom are said to be desolate spots on earth during the millennium (Isaiah 13:20-22; 34:5-15; Jeremiah 49:17,18; 50:39,40; 51:41-43) (from Fruchtenbaum, *Footsteps*, pp. 340–56).

Gog

The origin of the name *Gog* referred to in Ezekiel 38:2 is uncertain, though Ezekiel 38:2,3 states that Gog is the ruler of Magog and the "prince of Rosh, Meshech, and Tubal." *Gog* is either a title of the leader or a proper name. At some point following the rapture and before the middle of the tribulation, the armies and allies of Gog will launch an attack on Israel. The attackers will be repulsed and destroyed by supernatural intervention (Ezekiel 39:3).

Within pretribulationism there are differing views regarding the exact time of the attack. Some interpret the battle as occurring shortly after the rapture while others believe it will occur in the middle of the tribulation and, perhaps, carry on throughout the last three-and-a-half years. Whether we believe Gog leads armies against Israel in a single battle or a lengthy campaign, no one disputes the complete devastation of his forces. Ezekiel 38 and 39 graphically describe the demise of this military leader and his allies. Seven months will be required to bury the dead from the conflict (Ezekiel 39:11-15), and the weapons will provide enough fuel for Israel for seven years (Ezekiel 39:9,10).

TIMING OF THE BATTLE OF GOG & MAGOG

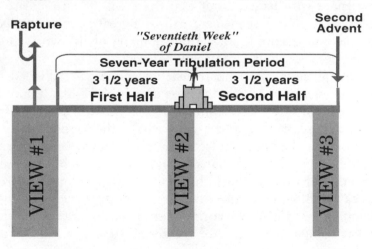

G

In Revelation 20:7-9, Gog and Magog are mentioned again, but even though common names are used, the battles are not the same. The timing and characteristics are very different.

See also "Magog."

Great Tribulation

The Bible distinguishes between the tribulation period (7 years) and the great tribulation (the final 3½ years). In Matthew 24:9 the word *tribulation* most likely refers to the full seven-year period of the tribulation. Matthew 24:21 speaks of the "great tribulation," which begins with the abomination of desolation that takes place after the midpoint of the seven-year period (Matthew 24:15).

Jesus told His disciples (in Matthew 24:15-20) that after the midpoint of the tribulation the Antichrist will break his covenant with Israel. After that there will be an increase in persecution: "For then there will be a great tribulation, such as has not occurred since the beginning of the world until now, nor ever shall" (Matthew 24:21).

Premillennial pretribulational interpreters are divided on how the term *great tribulation* is used in the Bible. It may be that the phrase "great tribulation" is a *technical* phrase referring to the last three-and-a-half years of the tribulation, or it is possible that the phrase is simply a *descriptive* term of those years. All agree that the Bible clearly teaches two segments, but does it label them differently? In other words, does the Bible label the first three-and-a-half years as "the tribulation" and the second three and a half years as "the great tribulation"? Or are the terms *tribulation* and *great tribulation* synonyms for the entire seven-year era?

Whichever interpretive preference is made, there *is no doctrinal orthodoxy or major interpretive issue at stake.* For either view, the basic seven-year, two-segment tribulation remains. What changes is *how* those two segments of three-and-a-half years are labeled. In a formula format, some understand—

Seven-year tribulation (3 1/2 years + 3 1/2 years) =
Great tribulation (3 1/2 years + 3 1/2 years)

and others understand—

Seven-year tribulation (3 1/2 years + 3 1/2 years) =
Tribulation (3 1/2 years) + great tribulation (3 1/2 years)

Regardless of the view taken, *both have a seven-year tribulation with two parts, and both recognize an increase in intensity during the last three-and-a-half years.*

Great White Throne

The phrase "great white throne" pertains to the judgment that is recorded in Revelation 20:11-15. There are several future judgments; this one is the judgment of the unbelieving dead at the end of the millennium. The Bible doesn't specifically state who sits on the throne, but it is probably Jesus Christ (as in Revelation 3:21). This judgment is the "resurrection of judgment" spoken of in John 5:29 (as opposed to the "resurrection of life"). All who experience this judgment are there because they have rejected Jesus Christ during their lifetimes. Because of their rejection of Christ's substitutionary work, God will judge them on the basis of their own works, which will utterly fail to measure up at any point to His holy standard. Their works are judged to show that the punishment is deserved. Everyone in this judgment is thrown into the lake of fire.

H

Hades

The New Testament Greek counterpart to the Hebrew term *Sheol* is hades. Hades was originally a proper noun in Greek—the name of the Greek god of the netherworld who ruled over the dead. In the New Testament, hades is used in two different ways. First, it can be used to describe a place when referring to punishment (Matthew 11:23; Luke 10:15; 16:23). Second, it can refer to the state of death which everyone experiences at the end of life (Matthew 16:18; Acts 2:27,31; Revelation 1:18; 6:8; 20:13,14). Hades is a temporary location whose occupants will eventually be cast into the lake of fire after the great white throne judgment.

See also "Sheol."

Harlot, Great

Just as Jesus Christ has His bride—the church—so Satan in his counterfeit program has his harlot (Revelation 17:1,15,16; 19:2). The great harlot represents all false religion, from the Tower of Babel in Genesis 11 to Revelation 17. The great harlot is associated with Babylon and the Antichrist because she is used by "the beast" to entice all earth dwellers, from kings to commoners, to follow the false ways of Satan.

Consistent with the character of a harlot, false religion projects outward beauty that is appealing to all who lack discernment, yet when examining its inner workings, it is easily seen to be lacking. Toward the end of the tribulation, the beast tires of his harlot and makes "her desolate and naked, and will eat her flesh and will burn her up with fire" (Revelation 17:16). The harlot is portrayed in Revelation 19:2 as responsible for the martyrdom of true believers in Christ.

This has been the role of religion gone astray. The great harlot becomes cruel and prosecutory as she strikes out against any who will not fornicate with her. Her destiny, along with all associates of Satan, is the lake of fire.

Heaven

In English translations of the Bible, there are more than 500 occurrences of the word *heaven*. Most of the verses use either the Hebrew word *shamayim*, which is literally translated "the heights," or the Greek word *ouranos*, which is literally translated "that which is raised up." These words are used throughout the Bible to refer to three different locations or realms: the atmosphere, the universe, and the abode of God. These three divisions have been recognized throughout history in both Christian and non-Christian sources, especially in classical Greek literature. While it is the third usage that we are primarily concerned with, all three usages are common in the Bible.

- *Atmospheric heaven*—Examples of this usage are seen in passages such as Deuteronomy 11:11,17; 28:12,24; Joshua 10:11; Psalm 18:13; 147:8; Proverbs 23:5; Isaiah 55:9,10; Zechariah 2:6; 6:5. Verses such as these emphasize the "first heaven" or the atmospheric realm.
- *Universe or celestial skies*—Examples of this usage are seen in passages such as Genesis 1:14; 15:5; Exodus 20:4; Psalm 33:6; Jeremiah 10:2: Hebrews 1:10. Frequently the celestial skies, or heavens, are used biblically in figures of speech such as hyperbole (Deuteronomy 1:28; 30:19; Daniel 4:11,20,22) or a metonymy which emphasizes totality (Deuteronomy 4:39; 30:19; Matthew 24:31; Colossians 1:23). It is also in this sense that we read of Jesus Christ's authority in Matthew 28:18-20.

- *Abode of God*—Examples of this usage are the primary focus of this study and are found in passages such as Psalm 33:13,14; Isaiah 63:15; Matthew 5:16,45; 6:1,9; 7:11,21; 10:32,33; 18:10; Revelation 3:12; 21:10. It is the abode of God, the "third heaven" that Paul speaks of in 2 Corinthians 12:2. This is the meaning Paul uses throughout his letters to the early churches. Jesus referred to heaven in this sense many times throughout His ministry.

Heaven is more than a mystical notion, imaginary dreamland, or philosophical concept. It is a real and present place in which God, the creator of all things, lives. Heaven is where Jesus came from at the incarnation, where He ascended after the resurrection, and from whence He will come again to receive all those who truly follow Him. It is the place the writer of Hebrews calls a "distant country" and for which those in his "hall of faith" longed (Hebrews 11:13-16).

Heaven is for all those who have obtained salvation based on the death of Jesus Christ. The souls of all believers enter heaven at the moment of death where, along with the Old Testament saints, they await their glorified resurrection bodies.

When a Christian dies, his or her spirit is immediately brought into heaven and the eternal presence of God. The Bible clearly teaches that when Christians die, they are instantaneously present with God. Paul writes of this in 2 Corinthians 5:6-8 and Philippians 1:23. In these passages there is no indication of any time lapse between death and entering heaven. Hebrews 12:23 also suggests that believers who have died are now in heaven without their resurrected bodies, awaiting the time when the body and soul will be united in a final, glorified state.

Jesus clearly promised the thief crucified beside Him that they would be together in paradise at the same moment and day (Luke 23:43). In Revelation 6:9-11, John writes of the disembodied souls of those people martyred during the early days of the tribulation crying out for divine justice. These verses show a consciousness of believers and presence with God.

Unbelievers are not and will not be in heaven. At the time of death, their bodies enter the grave and their souls enter hades to wait for the final judgment at the end of the millennium. Like believers, their bodies will one day be joined with their souls, but it will be for final judgment. They will not receive glorified bodies.

When we talk about heaven, we are referring to a location or place. When we speak of eternity we are talking about an era or eternal state. The eternal state is a yet-future dimension of time (without end). Heaven exists now even though we are not experiencing it, and it will continue to exist throughout eternity.

Hell

Hell is a place of eternal punishment and separation from God. The English word *hell* comes from a Teutonic root meaning "to hide" or "to cover" and is derived from the biblical Greek word and location *Gehenna*. Hell was created to accommodate Satan and the angels who rebelled with him against God (Matthew 25:41). The Bible refers to hell using several different words throughout the Old and New Testaments. Two of the clearest passages on hell in the New Testament are 2 Thessalonians 1:9 and Matthew 25:41,46. In 2 Thessalonians 1:9 Paul writes of those who reject God: "And these will pay the penalty of eternal destruction, away from the presence of the Lord and from the glory of His power." Jesus speaks of future judgment and hell in Matthew's gospel stating, "Then He will also say to those on His left, 'Depart from Me, accursed ones, into the eternal fire which has been prepared for the devil and his angels.' . . . And these will go away into eternal punishment, but the righteous into eternal life."

People who reject Jesus Christ and His free offer of salvation will join Satan in hell for eternity. Hell is a very real place, but the most important thing to know is that hell is *separation from God*. It is what people *choose* instead of accepting salvation through Jesus Christ. In the Bible, among the various words referring to or translated "hell" are: *Sheol, Hades, Gehenna*, and *Tartaros*.

Historicism

Historicism is one of four possible interpretive views regarding the role of timing in Bible prophecy. It addresses the interpretive question, "When will a prophecy be fulfilled in history?" The four views reflect the only four possibilities in relation to time: past (preterism), present (historicism), future (futurism), and timeless (idealism).

Historicism equates the current church age with the tribulation period through the day/year theory. The day/year theory takes numbers such as the 2,300 days (Daniel 8:14) and 1,290 days (Daniel 12:11) and declares them to be years. Thus, if one can find the right starting year it is merely a matter of adding the 2,300 or 1,290 years to discover the date of Christ's return. In addition, historicists also relate the seal, trumpet, and bowl judgments to major historical events for the last 2,000 years. For example, the fifth seal in Revelation 6 may be identified as the martyrdom under Roman Emperor Diocletian (A.D. 284–304). If that is true, then one might view the French Revolution as the first five bowl judgments of Revelation 16. This approach, coupled with the day/year theory naturally leads to date setting. Historicism was almost unanimously held by protestants from the Reformation to about 100 years ago. It is also the view of many of religious groups started in the nineteenth century, such as Mormonism, Seventh-day Adventism, and Jehovah Witnesses.

Equating the Roman Catholic institution and its popes with the Antichrist is another feature of historicism, so it is easy to understand why historicism is often called the protestant view. Most historicist schemes focus on European history, but there is a segment that replaces Europe with America. Some tend to see America as fulfilling the prophecies of Babylon. The following charts one historicist's interpretation of the book of Revelation.

Albert Barnes' Historical Interpretation of Revelation 6–19

ITEM	DESCRIPTION	BARNES' HISTORICAL INTERPRETATION
1st seal (Rev 6)	White horse— a conqueror	Peace and triumph in the Roman Empire from Domitian to Commodus (96-180)
2nd seal (Rev 6)	Red horse— war	Bloodshed from the death of Commodus onward (193-)
3rd seal (Rev 6)	Black horse— famine	Calamity in the time of Caracalla and onward (211-)
4th seal (Rev 6)	Green horse— death	Death by famine, etc., Decius to Callianus (243-268)
5th seal	Martyrs	Martyrdom under Diocletian (284-304)
6th seal (Rev 6)	Heavenly distrubances	Consternation at the threat of Barbarian invations, Goths, and Huns (365-)
1st trump (Rev 8)	$^1/_3$ earth smitten	Alaric and Goths invade the Western Roman Empire (395-410)
2nd trump (Rev 8)	$^1/_3$ sea smitten	Genseric and Vandals invade (4280468)
3rd trump (Rev 8)	$^1/_3$ rivers smitten	Attila and Huns invade (433-453)
4th trump (Rev 8)	$^1/_3$ sun, moon smitten	Odoacer and Heruli conquer Western Roman empire (476-490)
5th trump (Rev 8)	Torment of locusts	Mohometan and Saracen powers rise in the East (5 months of Rev 9:5—150 years)
6th trump (Rev 9)	horsemen slay $^1/_3$ men	Turkish power rises in the East

(continued)

Albert Barnes' Historical Interpretation of Revelation 6–19, *continued*

ITEM	DESCRIPTION	BARNES' HISTORICAL INTERPRETATION
Angel and little book (Rev 10)	Angel gives book to John	The Protestant Reformation. The 7 thunders of Rev 10:3,4—Papal false doctrine
The beast and false prophet (Rev 13)	They blaspheme 42 months	The evil career of ecclesiastical and civil Rome 42 montsh of Rev 13:5—1260 years!
First five bowls are poured out (Rev 16)	Wrath by sores; sea, rivers & sun smitten; darkness	The French Revolution and its aftermath strike at the Papcy
6th bowl of poured out (Rev 16)	Way prepared for armies to come to Armageddon	The frog like spirits call Paganism; Mohometanism, and Romanism prepare for their final struggle against the Gospel
7th bowl poured out (Rev 16)	Earthquake and hail; Babylon remembered for wrath	Papal power overthrown
Babylon destroyed (Rev 17-18)	Babylon destroyed	Destruction of Papal power
Battle of Armageddon (Rev 19)	Christ slays the beast and his armies	The Gospel finally triumphs morally over its foes who appear "as if" they're eaten by fowls

I

Idealism

Idealism is one of four possible interpretive views regarding the role of timing in Bible prophecy. It addresses the interpretive question, "When will a prophecy be fulfilled in history?" The four views reflect the only four possibilities in relation to time: past (preterism), present (historicism), future (futurism), and timeless (idealism).

In spite of the many statements in Bible prophecy that appear to deal with the timing of one event in relation to another, the idealist believes that either the Bible does not speak to these issues or we cannot know what it says. Idealists think that prophetic passages mainly teach that great ideas or truths about God and the Christian life are to be applied as timeless principles.

This nonliteral approach to prophecy is rarely held to by conservatives and evangelicals. Many liberals, who do not believe in a supernatural God who can predict the end from the beginning, favor this approach because of its elastic potential to make the text say virtually anything.

Imminency

Imminency in the New Testament teaches that Christ could return and rapture His church at any moment, without prior signs or warning. Dr. Renald Showers defines and describes imminence as follows:

1. An imminent event is one which is always "hanging overhead, is constantly ready to befall or overtake one; close at hand in its incidence" ("imminent," *The Oxford English Dictionary*, 1901, V, 66). Thus, imminence carries the sense that it could happen at any moment.

Other things *may* happen before the imminent event, but nothing else *must* take place before it happens. If something else must take place before an event can happen, then that event is not imminent. In other words, the necessity of something else taking place first destroys the concept of imminency.

2. Since a person never knows exactly when an imminent event will take place, then he cannot count on a certain amount of time transpiring before the imminent event happens. In light of this, he should always be prepared for it to happen at any moment.

3. A person cannot legitimately set or imply a date for its happening. As soon as a person sets a date for an imminent event he destroys the concept of imminency, because he thereby is saying that a certain amount of time must transpire before that event can happen. A specific date for an event is contrary to the concept that the event could happen at any moment.

4. A person cannot legitimately say that an imminent event will happen soon. The term "soon" implies that an event *must* take place "within a short time (after a particular point of time specified or implied)." By contrast, an imminent event *may* take place within a short time, but it does not *have* to do so in order to be imminent. As I hope you can see by now, "imminent" is not equal to "soon" (Showers, *Maranatha*, pp. 127-28).

The fact that Christ could return at any moment but may not soon is supported in the New Testament in the following passages: 1 Corinthians 1:7; 16:22; Philippians 3:20; 4:5; 1 Thessalonians 1:10; Titus 2:13; Hebrews 9:28; James 5:7-9; 1 Peter 1:13; Jude 21; Revelation 3:11; 22:7,12,17,20. These verses state that Christ could return at any moment—without warning—and instruct believers to wait and look for the Lord's coming.

As one considers the above list of passages, it becomes clear that Christ may come at any moment—that the rapture is actually imminent. Only pretribulationism can give a full, literal meaning to such an any-moment event. Other rapture views must redefine imminence more loosely than the New Testament allows.

The New Testament exhortation to be comforted by the Lord's coming (John 14:1; 1 Thessalonians 4:18) would no longer have meaning if believers first had to pass through any part of the tribulation; comfort would have to await passage through the events of the tribulation. Instead, the church has been given a "blessed hope," in part, because our Lord's return is truly imminent. In light of such admonitions, we should be always watching and waiting for His coming.

Israel

The study of Bible prophecy is divided into three major areas: Israel, the nations (Gentiles), and the church. Much detail is given prophetically concerning God's future plans for Israel. When we, as the church, take these prophecies to Israel literally, we see a great prophetic agenda that lies ahead for Israel as a people and nation. When the church spiritualizes these promises, as it has done too often in history, Israel's prophetic uniqueness is subsumed and merged unrealistically into the church. God has an amazing and blessed future for individual Jews and national Israel.

We have noted in previous entries (for example, see "Covenants") that God's promises to Abraham and Israel are unconditional and guaranteed through the various covenants. A definite pattern for Israel's future history was prophesied in Deuteronomy before the Jews set even one foot into the land (Deuteronomy 4; 28–31). The predicted pattern for God's program with Israel was to be as follows: They would enter the land under Joshua; they would eventually turn away from the Lord; they would be expelled from the land and scattered among the Gentile nations. From there, the Lord would regather them during the latter days, and they would pass through the tribulation. Toward the end of the tribulation they would be regenerated and recognize their Messiah. Christ then returns to earth and rescues Israel from the nations who have gathered at Armageddon to exterminate the Jews. A second regathering of the nation of Israel occurs in preparation for their millennial reign with Christ during which time all of Israel's unfulfilled promises will be realized. This pattern is developed by the prophets and reinforced by the New Testament.

As with the church and the nations, God is moving His chosen people—Israel—into place for the future completion of His program and their involvement after the rapture in direct fulfillment of prophecy. He has already brought them back to their ancient land and given them Jerusalem. However, the current situation in Israel is one of constant turmoil and crisis. This is preparation by God for Israel's signing of the covenant with the European Antichrist that will kick off the seven-year tribulation. Dr. John Walvoord provides the following prophetic checklist for Israel:

A Prophetic Checklist for Israel
1. The intense suffering and persecution of Jews throughout the world lead to pressure for a national home in Palestine.

2. Jews return to Palestine, and Israel is reestablished as a nation in 1948.

3. The infant nation survives against overwhelming odds.

4. Russia emerges as an important enemy of Israel, but the United States comes to the aid of Israel.

5. Israel's heroic survival and growing strength make it an established nation, recognized throughout the world.

6. Israel's military accomplishments become overshadowed by the Arabs' ability to wage a diplomatic war by controlling much of the world's oil reserves.

7. The Arab position is strengthened by their growing wealth and by alliances between Europe and key Arab countries.

8. The increasing isolation of the United States and Russia from the Middle East makes it more and more difficult for Israel to negotiate an acceptable peace settlement.

9. After a long struggle, Israel is forced to accept a compromise peace guaranteed by the new leader of the Mediterranean Confederacy of ten nations.

10. The Jewish people celebrate what appears to be a lasting and final peace settlement.

11. During three-and-a-half years of peace, Judaism is revived and traditional sacrifices and ceremonies are reinstituted in the rebuilt temple in Jerusalem.

12. The Russian army attempts to invade Israel but is mysteriously destroyed.

13. The newly proclaimed world dictator desecrates the temple in Jerusalem and begins a period of intense persecution of Jews.

14. Many Jews recognize the unfolding of prophetic events and declare their faith in Christ as the Messiah of Israel.

15. In the massacre of Jews and Christians who resist the world dictator, some witnesses are divinely preserved to carry the message throughout the world.
16. Christ returns to earth, welcomed by believing Jews as their Messiah and deliverer.
17. Christ's thousand-year reign on earth from the throne of David finally fulfills the prophetic promises to the nations of Israel.

The many items listed above individually constitute specific signs that God's end-time program is on the verge of springing into full gear. Additionally, the fact that all three streams of prophecy (nations, Israel, and the church) are converging for the first time in history constitutes a sign in and of itself. This is why many students of prophecy believe we are on the edge of history. If you want to know where history is headed, keep your eye on what God is doing with Israel.

Israel, Dispersion of

The Latin word *diaspora* has been adapted to refer to Israel's dispersion throughout the Gentile nations. Christ speaks of the current 2,000-year dispersion of Israel in His prophecy about the destruction of Jerusalem in A.D. 70: "And they will fall by the edge of the sword, and will be led captive into all the nations; and Jerusalem will be trampled under foot by the Gentiles until the times of the Gentiles be fulfilled" (Luke 21:24). As usual within biblical prophecy, the pronouncement of judgment also contains an ultimate hope of restoration. In this passage Christ said "until," which means the dispersion will not last forever.

As early as the Mosaic law, the threat of dispersion throughout the nations was spoken of (Leviticus 26:33; Deuteronomy

4:27; 28:64; 29:28). Nehemiah said, "Remember the word which Thou didst command Thy servant Moses saying, 'If you are unfaithful I will scatter you among the peoples'" (Nehemiah 1:8). This is repeated many times by the prophets.

Israel's capture of the Northern Kingdom by the Assyrians in the eighth century B.C. and the trip to Babylon in the sixth century B.C. did not constitute a worldwide scattering as prophesied. This did not occur until the nation's rejection of Christ and God's subsequent judgment in A.D. 70.

We rejoice that God is currently in the process of ending the diaspora. May it happen soon!

Israel, Regathering and Conversion of

There are dozens of biblical passages that predict an end-time regathering of the Israelites back to their land. However, it is a common mistake to lump all of these passages into one fulfillment timeframe—especially in relation to the modern state of Israel. Modern Israel is prophetically significant and is fulfilling Bible prophecy. Readers of God's Word need to be careful to distinguish which verses are being fulfilled in our day and which references await future events. In short, there will be *two* end-time regatherings—one before the tribulation and one after the tribulation.

Hebrew Christian scholar Dr. Arnold Fruchtenbaum explains:

> The reestablishment of the Jewish state in 1948 has not only thrown a wrench in amillennial thinking, but it has also thrown a chink in much of premillennial thinking. Amazingly, some premillennialists have concluded that the present state of Israel has nothing to do with the fulfillment of prophecy. For some reason the present state somehow does not fit their scheme of things, and so the present state becomes merely an

accident of history. On what grounds is the present state of Israel so dismissed? The issue that bothers so many premillennialists is the fact that not only have the Jews returned in unbelief with regard to the person of Jesus, but the majority of the ones who have returned are not even Orthodox Jews. In fact the majority are atheists or agnostics. Certainly, then, Israel does not fit in with all those biblical passages dealing with the return. For it is a regenerated nation that the Bible speaks of, and the present state of Israel hardly fits that picture. So on these grounds, the present state is dismissed as not being a fulfillment of prophecy.

However, the real problem is the failure to see that the prophets spoke of two international returns. First, there was to be a regathering in unbelief in preparation for judgment, namely the judgment of the tribulation. This was to be followed by a second worldwide regathering in faith in preparation for blessing, namely the blessings of the messianic age. Once it is recognized that the Bible speaks of two such regatherings, it is easy to see how the present state of Israel fits into prophecy (*Footsteps*, p. 65).

First Worldwide Gathering in Unbelief In 1948 when the modern state of Israel was born, it not only became an important stage-setting development but also began an actual fulfillment of specific Bible prophecies about an international regathering of the Jews before the judgment of the tribulation. This "regathering in unbelief" prediction is found in the following Old Testament passages: Ezekiel 20:33-38; 22:17-22; 36:22-24; Isaiah 11:11,12; Zephaniah 2:1,2. Ezekiel 38–39 presupposes such a regathering.

Zephaniah 1:14-18 is one of the most colorful descriptions of "The day of the Lord," which we commonly call the

ISRAEL'S TWO END-TIME
REGATHERINGS TO THE LAND

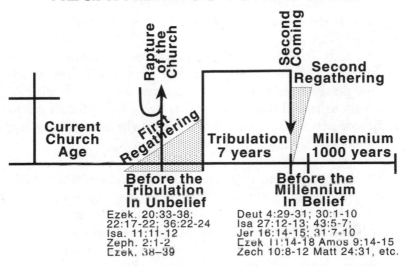

Before the
Tribulation
In Unbelief
Ezek. 20:33-38;
22:17-22; 36:22-24
Isa. 11:11-12
Zeph. 2:1-2
Ezek. 38-39

Before the
Millennium
In Belief
Deut 4:29-31; 30:1-10
Isa 27:12-13; 43:5-7;
Jer 16:14-15; 31:7-10
Ezek 11:14-18 Amos 9:14-15
Zech 10:8-12 Matt 24:31, etc.

tribulation period. Zephaniah 2:1,2 says that there will be a
worldwide regathering of Israel before the day of the Lord:

Gather yourselves together, yes, gather, O nation without
shame, before the decree takes effect—the day passes like the
chaff—before the burning anger of the LORD comes upon
you, before the day of the LORD's anger comes upon you.

Second Worldwide Gathering in Belief   Many biblical passages speak of Israel's regathering in belief at the end of the
tribulation in conjunction with Christ's second coming and
in preparation for the commencement of the millennium.

These references are not being fulfilled by the modern state of Israel. Some of these citations are: Deuteronomy 4:29-31; 30:1-10; Isaiah 27:12,13; 43:5-7; Jeremiah 16:14,15; 31:7-10; Ezekiel 11:14-18; Amos 9:14,15; Zechariah 10:8-12; Matthew 24:31.

The fact that the last 50 years has seen a worldwide re-gathering and reestablishment of the nation of Israel, which is now poised in just the setting required for the revealing of the Antichrist and the start of the tribulation, is God's grand indicator that all of the other areas of world development are prophetically significant. Dr. Walvoord says,

> Of the many peculiar phenomena which characterize the present generation, few events can claim equal significance as far as Biblical prophecy is concerned with that of the return of Israel to their land. It constitutes a preparation for the end of the age, the setting for the coming of the Lord for His church, and the fulfillment of Israel's prophetic destiny (*Israel in Prophecy,* p. 26).

Israel, God's "super-sign" of the end times, is a clear indicator that time is growing short. God is preparing the world for the final events leading up to Israel's national regeneration.

J

Jerusalem

The city of Jerusalem has a definite role in God's plan for the future. Scripture clearly teaches that the covenant of territory made with Abraham, which includes Jerusalem, was an unconditional promise. The Bible contains many prophecies about Jerusalem, some of the most extensive and clearest ones are Isaiah 60–61; Zechariah 12 and 14; and Revelation 21–22.

Jerusalem will experience both war and peace during the tribulation. It has always been a city whose daily life swings as a pendulum between these two conditions. In the tribulation, the pendulum will swing even faster and there will be extensive political and religious activity in Jerusalem. The Antichrist will be very active in the city and the fortunes of the city will turn from prosperity to persecution. It is reasonable to deduce from Scripture that Antichrist will establish Jerusalem as his new capital. The Antichrist will be closely associated with the city, but that relationship will not endure and, ultimately, the inhabitants of Jerusalem will recognize the true Messiah.

We know from Daniel 9:27 that the Antichrist will make a political covenant with Israel. For the first three-and-a-half years of the tribulation there will be some degree of political stability in Jerusalem and Israel, but this will eventually be shattered by the Antichrist as he transforms his image to include that of a religious leader. After the first half of the tribulation the Antichrist will break the covenant of peace he has made with Israel, and intense persecution and suffering will occur in Jerusalem and throughout the world. This oppression will culminate in the battle of Armageddon, during which Jerusalem will be a focal point (Zechariah 12:2-4).

In the first half of the tribulation there will be peace in the city, although other disasters will befall it from the seal and trumpet judgments of Revelation 6, 8, and 9. At the midpoint of the tribulation, the Antichrist will desecrate the temple, stop any worship in it, and begin to persecute the Jews in Jerusalem. This marks the beginning of the last half of the tribulation that Jesus prophesied of in Matthew 24:15-22. At this time, Jews living in Jerusalem are told to flee immediately from the city and go into the hills.

At some point during the tribulation, Israel will experience the fighting and events of Ezekiel 38–39, when armies from Gog and Magog will come against the nation. These forces will be destroyed by God through natural disaster and internal dissension (Ezekiel 38:17-23).

In the second half of the tribulation, the city will experience war, especially at the end as the battle of Armageddon ensues. According to Zechariah 14:1-3, armies will be fighting in Jerusalem on the very day of the second coming of Christ. Under attack, Israel will receive supernatural strength and the Israelites will be victorious (Zechariah 12:8,9).

At the end of the tribulation, a critical time in both Jerusalem's history and humanity's history, Jesus the Messiah will return to the Mount of Olives in Jerusalem. He will destroy His enemies that have assembled in military force at Armageddon (Zechariah 14:2-4,8,9). Also, when Jesus Christ returns, Jerusalem and Israel will acknowledge Him as the Messiah (Zechariah 12:10). Isaiah 60–61 describes the glory of Jerusalem and Israel during the millennium and the ministry of Jesus during this period. It is during this time that Jerusalem will finally be a true city of peace (Isaiah 60:17,18).

It will be from Jerusalem that Jesus Christ will establish a theocracy and reign throughout the millennium. Beginning in Jerusalem, there will be universal justice and peace (Isaiah

2:34; 11:2-5). Jeremiah recorded God's promises of this era that a Messiah-King would emerge from the Davidic dynasty and rule in righteousness and justice (Jeremiah 33:15,16). For 1,000 years Jerusalem will know peace and prosperity under the benevolent and righteous rule of Jesus Christ. All aspects of daily life will be affected as glory dwells in Immanuel's land from the Holy City. At the end of the millennium, God will carry forth the beloved name of Jerusalem as the name associated with His glory and presence.

The new Jerusalem of Revelation 3:12 and 21,22 (also Hebrews 11:8-10; 12:22-25) will descend from heaven and continue through eternity. It will be the dwelling place of the redeemed of all ages who will serve God eternally (Revelation 22:3). The new Jerusalem will be a city of joy whose gates will never be closed. Ultimately it will be a city of purity inhabited only by believers (Revelation 21:25-27). The new Jerusalem will be your eternal dwelling place if you are a believer in Jesus Christ.

See also "New Jerusalem."

Jesus Christ

Jesus Christ is the focus and goal of all history (Ephesians 1:10; Romans 11:36). History is moving toward the ultimate visible reign of Christ on earth (in the millennium) and for eternity (in the "new Jerusalem"). There is much that could be noted about Jesus Christ and Bible prophecy. Dr. John Walvoord has noted:

> Theologians have often pointed out that Jesus Christ is the center of theology because all the great purposes of God depend on Him—His person and His works. What is true of theology as a whole is especially true of eschatology. Biblical

prophecies about Jesus Christ begin in Genesis with the Garden of Eden and climax in the last book of the Bible, with its theme "The Revelation of Jesus Christ" (Revelation 1:1). Accordingly, while prophecy in its broad revelation deals with such great scenes as the history of the world, the divine program of God for Israel, and His plan for the church, central in all these great themes is Jesus Christ, the Savior, the ultimate judge of all men, the final victor over sin and death. All prophecy, whatever its theme, is ultimately connected in some way or other to the purposes of God in and through Christ (*Prophecy: 14 Essential Keys,* p. 20).

Dr. H. L. Willmington has collected and listed all the names of Christ used in Revelation. This points us to the fact that all prophecy focuses on Jesus, the Christ:

- Jesus Christ (1:1)
- Faithful witness (1:5)
- First begotten of the dead (1:5)
- Prince of the kings of the earth (1:5)
- Alpha and Omega (1:8)
- Son of man (1:13)
- First and the last (1:17)
- Son of God (2:18)
- Keeper of the keys of hell and death (1:18)
- Keeper of David's keys (3:7)
- Lion of the tribe of Judah (5:5)
- Root of David (5:5)
- Slain Lamb (5:6)
- Angry Lamb (6:16,17)
- Tender Lamb (7:17)
- Our Lord (11:8)
- Man child (12:5)

- King of saints (15:3)
- Faithful and True (19:11)
- Word of God (19:13)
- King of kings (19:16)
- Lord of lords (19:16)
- Beginning and the End (22:13)
- Bright and morning star (22:16)

(*Willmington's Guide,* pp. 275–76)

Since Jesus Christ is both God and man, He relates to heaven and earth in a way no other one can. He is the second Adam, the ultimate prophet, priest, and king. He currently is the head of the church, seated at the right hand of the Father. When He returns, He will take His rightful seat upon the throne of David as Israel's messianic ruler. Jesus is the culmination of all things. This is why Christ, and Christ alone, is worthy of the statement spoken by the disciple Thomas: "My Lord and my God!" (John 20:28).

Jews

Jew has developed into a term that designates a Hebrew or Israelite. The English word *Jew* is derived from the biblical word *Judah*. Before the Babylonian captivity of the sixth century B.C., the term referred exclusively to those who were of the tribe of Judah. However, in the return to Israel under the Persians the greatest percentage of people were from the tribe of Judah. It was during this time that *Jew* became a designation for anyone from the 12 tribes of Israel. *Jew* is used in this way in the New Testament and has been, perhaps, the most common designation of Israel up to and including our own day.

See also "Israel."

J

Judgment Day

There are several times of judgment in the future, each with a specific purpose, end, and constituency. To speak of a single, all-encompassing judgment day is incorrect. There are different judgments for believers' works, Old Testament saints, tribulation saints, living Jews at the end of the tribulation, living Gentiles at the end of the tribulation, Satan and the fallen angels, and unredeemed people.

THE COMING JUDGMENTS AND RESURRECTIONS

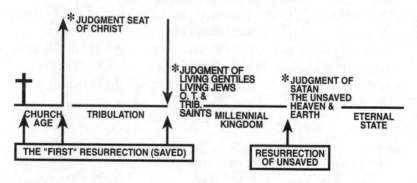

Judgment Seat of Christ

Paul told the Corinthian believers, "We must all appear before the judgment seat [bema] of Christ, that each one may be recompensed for his deeds in the body, according to what he has done, whether good or bad" (2 Corinthians 5:10). In Romans, Paul notes that "we shall all stand before the judgment seat [bema] of God" (Romans 14:10). This event is the judgment of evaluation that only church-age believers will undergo.

It is not the same as the judgment that unbelievers will undergo before the great white throne (Revelation 20:11-15).

See also "Bema."

Judgments

Though we often hear the phrase "judgment day," it is not biblically accurate because there are several future judgments in God's prophetic plan. These judgments will occur at various times between the rapture and the end of the millennium. The judgments are certain; no one will escape them. They will make manifest God's justice and righteousness to all the world and will silence all who have scoffed at or denied God. The chart on page 120 provides a comparison of the judgments.

Judgments, Tribulation

In the book of Revelation, there are three tribulation judgments: seals, trumpets, and bowls. At first glance, one might believe that these judgments are different from one another and occur in the sequence presented in the text. However, a few prophecy teachers believe that the seal, trumpet, and bowl judgments are not 21 separate judgments but, instead, are 7 events that are repeated 3 times, first as seals, second as trumpets, third as bowls.

The order of the seal, trumpet, and bowl judgments should be understood sequentially for the following reasons: 1) This is the order in which they appear in the text, and there are no specific reasons to suggest that they should be taken in a way different from how they are presented. 2) The details of each judgment are significantly different so it is impossible to explain how each is a restatement of another. 3) Out of the seventh seal arises the next set of judgments, while the seventh

J

JUDGMENT	TIME	PLACE	PERSONS	BASIS	RESULTS	SCRIPTURE
Believers' Works	Between Rapture and Second Coming	*Bema* of Christ	Believers in Christ	Works and walk of the Christian life	Rewards or loss of rewards	1 Cor. 3:10-15; 2 Cor. 5:10
Old Testament Saints	End of Tribulation/ Second Coming		Believers in O.T. times	Faith in God	Rewards	Dan. 12:1-3
Tribulation Saints	End of Tribulation/ Second Coming		Believers of Tribulation period	Faith in and faithful- ness to Chirst	Reign with with Chirst in the Millennium	Rev. 20:4-6
Living Jews	End of Tribulation/ Second Coming	Wilder- ness	Jews who survive the Tribulation	Faith in Christ	Believers enter kingdom; rebels are purged	Ezek. 20:34-38
Living Gentiles	End of Tribulation/ Second Coming	Valley of Jehosha- phat	Gentiles who survive the Tribulation	Faith in Christ as proved by works	Believers enter the kingdom; others go to lake of fire	Joel 3:1,2; Matt. 25:31-46
Satan and Fallen Angels	End of Millennium		Satan and those angels who follow him	Allegiance to Satan's counterfeit system	Lake of fire	Matt. 25:41; 2 Peter 2:4; Jude 6; Rev. 20:10
Unsolved People	End of Millennium	Before the Great White Throne	Unbelievers of all time	Rejection to God	Lake of filre	Rev. 20:11-15

(Ryrie, *Basic Theology,* p. 516. Used by permission).

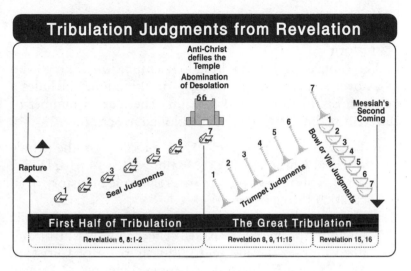

Tribulation Judgments from Revelation

Anti-Christ
defiles the
Temple

Abomination
of Desolation

Messiah's
Second
Coming

Rapture

Seal Judgments

Trumpet Judgments

Bowl or Vial Judgments

First Half of Tribulation	The Great Tribulation	
Revelation 6, 8:1-2	Revelation 8, 9, 11:15	Revelation 15, 16

bowl is an actual judgment. The seven judgments cannot be harmonized within a recapitulation framework. 4) Ordinal numbers are used in each sequence (first, second, third), which indicate succession and not repetition.

In summary, the specific textual details can only be harmonized if they occur successively.

K

Kingdom

The biblical words for kingdom emphasize a king who rules over something. The concept of "kingdom" includes a ruler, those ruled over, and a realm. There are a number of different realms or kingdoms mentioned in Scripture:

- The *universal* kingdom—God as ruler of the whole world (1 Chronicles 29:11; Psalm 96:13; 145:13; Daniel 2:37). This refers to God's sovereign rule of history from creation through eternity.
- The *Davidic/Messianic* kingdom—This is the Davidic kingdom promised to Israel. The promise will be fulfilled only in the future 1,000-year reign of Christ on earth during His earthly millennial kingdom (2 Samuel 7:12-16; Revelation 20:1-10).
- The *mystery* form of the kingdom—Secrets (that is, previously unrevealed information) about a kingdom which will encompass the period between the two advents of Christ (often known as Christendom) (Matthew 13).
- The *spiritual* kingdom—Refers to God's rule over His people at all times in history. There is never a time when this kingdom is not in operation.
- The kingdom of *man*—Began after the flood in Babylon through the Tower of Babel incident (Genesis 10, 11). Throughout Scripture, Babylon is the focus of opposition to God. This is why Israel is carried off into the Babylonian captivity and why, during the future tribulation, the Antichrist's world empire is associated with Babylon (Revelation 17, 18). God's judgment of the kingdom of man at the end of history is needed in preparation for the establishment of the messianic kingdom (Revelation 19–20).

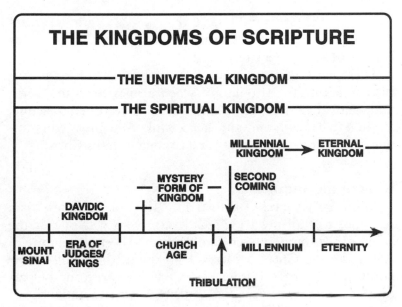

THE KINGDOMS OF SCRIPTURE

THE UNIVERSAL KINGDOM

THE SPIRITUAL KINGDOM

MILLENNIAL KINGDOM → ETERNAL KINGDOM

MYSTERY FORM OF KINGDOM

SECOND COMING

DAVIDIC KINGDOM

MOUNT SINAI | ERA OF JUDGES/ KINGS | CHURCH AGE | MILLENNIUM | ETERNITY

TRIBULATION

Kingdom of God

Much debate has surrounded the meaning of the term "kingdom of God." As noted in the "Kingdom" entry, there are multiple realms mentioned in the Bible. We believe that most of the time the phrase "kingdom of God" in the Bible is a reference to Messiah's earthly, millennial kingdom that will occur at Christ's second coming.

King of the North

"The king of the North," found in the early verses of Daniel 11, refers to several individuals: Ptolemy II (285–246 B.C.), Seleucus II Callinicus (247–226 B.C.), and Ptolemy III (246–221 B.C.), who battled Seleucus II. After the death of

Alexander the Great (323 B.C.), there was a continual struggle between the dynasties of the Ptolemies and Seleucids for control of Alexander's territory.

These early verses prefigure the struggle against the Antichrist during the tribulation when armies from the north and south align themselves against him as recorded in Daniel 11:40-45. Though initially successful, Antichrist will ultimately be defeated at the second coming of Jesus Christ.

King of the South

In the early verses of Daniel 11, "King of the South" is a reference to Ptolemy I (323–285 B.C), who was one of the rulers of the southern section of what had been the empire of Alexander the Great. Ptolemy I prefigures the "king of the South" spoken of in Daniel 11:40, who will arise and be part of a coalition force that will come against the Antichrist at some point during the tribulation. The attack from the south will coincide with a similar attack from the "king of the North" (Daniel 11:40). The Antichrist will defeat these forces, thereby increasing his international power and control.

Kings of the East

Revelation 16:12 says, ". . . that the way might be prepared for the kings from the east." There are many interpretations of the phrase "kings from the east" and much speculation as to who these kings will be. What is known for sure is that rulers from the east will march against Israel in the campaign of Armageddon. In the Bible, "the east," as oriented in reference to the land of Israel, always refers to Mesopotamia and Assyria (Babylon). The fact that the Antichrist's capital will be Babylon, which sits on the banks of the Euphrates River, further enhances the interpretation of the kings as being Mesopotamian. These forces will be part of the great alliance put together by the Antichrist to attempt to crush Israel. This is not the same as the 200-million-strong army of demonic beings mentioned Revelation 9:16. (The 200 million figure occurs in the *sixth trumpet judgment*.) In Revelation 16:12, the reference is to activity in the *sixth bowl judgment*. At this time the Euphrates River will be supernaturally dried up, which will assist the armies on their march toward their final destruction by God at Armageddon.

L

Lake of Fire

The phrase "lake of fire" appears five times in the New Testament, all in Revelation (19:20; 20:14,15; 21:8). It is one of several biblical terms or phrases used in relation to hell and the eternal punishment of unbelievers and enemies of God, including Satan, the beast, and the False Prophet. According to Revelation 20:11-15, unbelievers will be cast into the lake of fire after the great white throne judgment and remain there forever.

At our present time in history, no one is in the lake of fire. However, the current residence of all dead unbelievers since the beginning of creation is called "Sheol" in the Old Testament and "hades" or "hell" in the New Testament. According to Luke 16, this place is very much *like* the lake of fire, but it is not the same. This can be compared to a prisoner who is kept in the county jail until after his trial and sentencing, at which time he is transported to serve out his time in the state or federal penitentiary. The county jail is not the same place as the penitentiary, but they are very similar. So it is that the current abode of the lost is not yet in the lake of fire, but their current residence in hell is similar. After the great white throne judgment, all fallen angels and the lost of humanity will spend eternity in the lake of fire. Believers, however, will enter heaven and eternal life in the presence of God.

Lamb of God

This is a title given to the Lord Jesus Christ in John 1:29,36 in His first coming. It draws heavily on the imagery of the Passover lamb (Exodus 12:3) and the messianic prophecy of Isaiah 53, especially verse 7. The passages liken Christ to a sacrificial lamb who patiently and innocently endures death to expiate sin. The imagery appears again in Revelation 5:6,12 and 12:11, referring to Jesus Christ. "Lamb" is one of more than 20 names used for Jesus in Revelation.

In these passages Jesus Christ, as the slain Lamb of God who died to pay the penalty of human sin, is worthy of universal honor and praise. This homage and worship is due to Him not only because of what He did but also because of who He is as the second member of the trinity. In His first coming and in His death, Jesus Christ was like a lamb. In His second coming, He will be like a lion in that He will be sovereign, majestic, and exercising great power (see Revelation 5:5).

M

Magog

Magog is the territory under the rule of Gog as described in Ezekiel 38–39. According to the historian Josephus, Magog was the land of the nomadic Scythians, the region north and northeast of the Black Sea and east of the Caspian Sea. The area would have included territory that is occupied today by Russia, the Ukraine, and Kazakhstan. Ezekiel 38:2 also speaks of Gog as the prince of Rosh, Meshech, and Tubal. These entities could be either components of Magog or allies. Some Bible versions have also translated Rosh, not as a proper name, but as "chief." Dr. Edwin Yamauchi writes of Magog and the others:

> Though the identification of Gog and Magog still remains disputed, the identifications of Meshech and Tubal have for a long time not been in doubt. . . . The association with Moscow and Tobolsk is untenable. . . . Since the late nineteenth century, Assyrian texts have been available which locate Mushku (Meshech) and Tabal (Tubal) in central and eastern Anatolia [Turkey] respectively (Yamauchi, *Foes from the Northern Frontier,* pp. 24-25).

According to Ezekiel 38:5,6, joining Magog in the struggle against Israel will be Persia (Iran), Ethiopia (Cush), Put (Libya), Gomer (eastern Turkey), and Beth-togarmah (northwestern Turkey or Azerbaijan). The forces of Gog will come from the north and the south against Israel during the tribulation; they will be supernaturally defeated by God.

See also "Gog."

Man of Lawlessness

This is a descriptive term and title used by Paul in 2 Thessalonians 2:3 to describe the Antichrist. In verse 8, he is referred to as "that lawless one." It is only one of many biblical terms used as a synonym for the Antichrist. Lawlessness stresses his rebellious nature and deeds. Whatever law God makes he is sure to break it. Apparently he will be the most lawless creature in history. His rebellion is directed against God and His law.

See also "Antichrist."

Man of Sin

"Man of sin" comes from 2 Thessalonians 2:3 (KJV) and refers to the Antichrist who will arise during the tribulation. This is one of the many names by which he is called in Scripture. Each name brings out an aspect of his infamous character. This title informs us that he personifies sin or lawlessness. His every act is rebellion against God. In the NASB and NIV, the phrase is translated "man of lawlessness."

See also "Man of Lawlessness."

Maranatha

Maranatha was a greeting often used in the first-century church, as recorded in 1 Corinthians 16:22. Maranatha consists of three Aramaic words: *Mar* ("Lord"), *ana* ("our"), and *tha* ("come"), meaning "our Lord, come." The use of this greeting among fellow believers in the ancient church clearly reflected the eager expectation and hope they had that the Lord could come for them at any moment. They lived in light of this expectation just as we are supposed to in our day.

Mark of the Beast

The mark of the beast is mentioned in Revelation 13:16,17; 14:9; and 20:4. According to the first of these passages, during the tribulation everyone will be required to receive the mark or the name of the beast before "buying or selling," that is, before they can conduct any normal daily business. All private and public transactions will require that the parties involved have this mark. Those who do not have it will be subject to great difficulty and persecution. To take the mark will signify one's commitment and devotion to the Antichrist and affirm one's belief that Satan is the supreme deity. The mark will be a visible symbol of the immense power and worldwide authority of the Antichrist.

Thousands of people will refuse to receive the mark and, according to Revelation 20:2-4, they will be beheaded. However, they will be resurrected at the second coming to reign with Christ in the millennium. Clearly, with today's technology, a future world ruler who is in complete control would have the ability to know which people had pledged their allegiance to him and received the mark and which people had not received it.

The biblical word for *mark* is similar to our modern "tattoo" or "brand." Throughout the Bible, the word for *mark* is employed to distinguish or indicate something by a sign. For example, it is used many times in Leviticus as a reference to a mark which renders the subject ceremonially unclean, usually related to leprosy. In Ezekiel 9:4 there is a use of *mark* similar to the way it is used in Revelation: "And the LORD said to him, 'Go through the midst of the city, even through the midst of Jerusalem, and put *a mark on the foreheads* of the men who sigh and groan over all the abominations which are being committed in its midst'" (emphasis added). Here was a mark of preservation similar to the way the blood on the doorposts spared the Israelites from the death angel (Exodus 12:21-30). In Ezekiel the mark is placed on the forehead, which anticipates Revelation's use of the term.

All seven instances of the Greek word for *sign, charagma,* in the Greek New Testament appear in Revelation, and all refer to "the mark of the beast" (Revelation 13:16,17; 14:9,11; 16:2; 19:20; 20:4). Dr. Robert Thomas explains how the word was used in ancient times:

> The mark must be some sort of branding similar to that given soldiers, slaves, and temple devotees in John's day. In Asia Minor, devotees of pagan religions delighted in the display of such a tattoo as an emblem of ownership by a certain god. In Egypt, Ptolemy Philopator I branded Jews, who submitted to registration, with an ivy leaf in recognition of their Dionysian worship (cf. 3 Maccabees 2:29). This meaning resembles the long-time practice of carrying signs to advertise religious loyalties (cf. Isaiah 44:5) and follows the habit of branding slaves with the name or special mark of their owners (cf. Galatians 6:17). *Charagma* ("Mark") was a term for the images or names of emperors on Roman coins, so it fittingly could apply to the beast's emblem put on people (Thomas, *Revelation,* 8–22, p. 181).

The Antichrist's mark appears to be a parody of the plan of God, especially God's "sealing" of the 144,000 witnesses of Revelation 7. God's seal of His witnesses most likely is invisible and for the purpose of protection from the Antichrist. The Greek word for *seal* is a totally different term than the word for *mark.* On the other hand, Antichrist offers protection from the wrath of God—a promise he cannot deliver on—and the mark is external. Since those receiving the mark of the beast take it willingly, it must be a point of pride to have, in essence, Satan as one's owner. The term

M

mark denotes "loyalty, ownership, and protection, just as the seal given the slaves of God. The verb (*charassô*, 'I engrave') is the source of *charagma* (cf. Acts 17:29). It will be visible and the point of recognition for all in subjection to the beast"(Thomas, *Revelation, 8–22*, p. 181).

The Bible speaks precisely about what the mark will be:

- the Antichrist's mark, identified with his person
- the actual number 666, not a representation
- a mark, like a tattoo
- visible to the naked eye
- on the person, not in him or her
- recognized, not questioned
- voluntary, not involuntary—not given through stealth or trickery
- used after the rapture, not before
- used in the second half of the tribulation
- needed to buy and sell
- universally received by non-Christians, but universally rejected by Christians
- a show of worship and allegiance to the Antichrist
- promoted by the False Prophet
- the mark that leads to eternal punishment in the lake of fire

The Antichrist will attempt to mimic the importance, rule, and work of Christ in many ways and this is one of them. In that regard, it is interesting to note the words of the apostle Paul in Galatians 6:17: "From now on let no one cause trouble for me, for I bear on my body the brand-marks of Jesus."

Marriage of the Lamb

Scripture indicates that the Lamb (Jesus Christ) will be married to the church in Ephesians 5:25-32. After the rapture of the church to heaven and during the tribulation, the church, as a "bride," prepares for marriage by adorning herself in a white linen garment, which is said to be the righteous acts of the saints (Revelation 19:8). The "linen garment" comes from the bema or judgment seat of Christ by which the church is evaluated and receives rewards that become her adornment for the wedding.

The apostle Paul likely is the best man because he says, "For I betrothed you to one husband, that to Christ I might present you as a pure virgin" (2 Corinthians 11:2). The church is presented to Christ as a whole, which means she must be prepared as a unit in heaven during the tribulation. Revelation 19:7 says, "Let us rejoice and be glad and give the glory to Him, for the marriage of the Lamb has come and His bride has made herself ready."

Marriage Supper of the Lamb

Revelation 19:9 says, "Blessed are those who are invited to the marriage supper of the Lamb." This supper is a celebration of marriage, much as we have today in the form of a reception or dinner after the ceremony. This will certainly be an occasion for celebration.

Some speculate that this event will occur during the 75-day interval between the second coming and the start of the millennium that is mentioned in Daniel 12:11,12. However, it seems to make better sense to see the supper taking place in the millennium itself. Jesus said in Luke 22:18 concerning the Lord's supper, "I will not drink of the fruit of the vine from now on until the kingdom of God comes."

Messianic Kingdom

Many of the Old Testament prophets spoke extensively of the messianic kingdom. They viewed it as a time when

M

Messiah will be present in the nation of Israel and will have defeated Israel's enemies. All will be well with the nation because Messiah will finally be there. The messianic kingdom is the same entity as the arrival of the Davidic kingdom, the kingdom of God, and the millennium of Revelation 20. Some of the major Old Testament references include: Psalm 15; 24; Isaiah 2:2,3; 11:6-9; 65:17-25; Micah 4:1-5.

Dr. Arnold Fruchtenbaum summarizes the messianic kingdom:

> To summarize the general characteristics of the messianic kingdom, it will be a time when Satan will be bound, causing a reduction of both sin and death though neither of these two will be eliminated at that time. It will be a time of universal and personal prosperity and peace between man and man, between animal and animal, and between man and animal, with many of the effects (but not all) of the curse removed. It will be a time characterized by truth, holiness and righteousness with justice continually being dispersed from Jerusalem. It will be a time of labor in building and planting with guaranteed results and promised enjoyment of these labors (*Footsteps*, p. 274).

See also "Millennium."

Michael

Michael is an archangel, that is, the first among the angels in rank. The name Michael literally means "who is like God" and is a stark contrast with the fallen angel Satan who declared, "I will make myself like the Most High"(Isaiah 14:14). Interpreters are divided on whether there is only one archangel or more than one, but even if there is more than one archangel, Michael is the most prominent (Daniel

10:13,21; 12:1; Jude 9; Revelation 12:7). Daniel explicitly identifies Michael as a prince and guardian of the nation of Israel (Daniel 10:21; 12:1). Michael will be especially prominent during the last half of the tribulation, Israel's "time of distress" (Daniel 12:1; Jeremiah 30:7; Matthew 24:21).

Midtribulationism

This view teaches that all believers will be taken in the rapture at some point around the middle (after the first three-and-a-half years) of the tribulation.

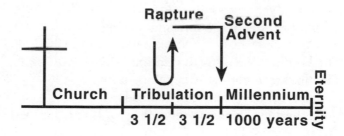

MIDTRIBULATIONAL RAPTURE

See also "Pretribulationism" and "Posttribulationism."

Millennial Kingdom

The millennial kingdom is merely another term for the more widely used expression "millennium." The word "kingdom" emphasizes the political nature of Christ's future realm which will last 1,000 years (Revelation 20:1-7).

Millennium

Millennium is a Latin term for "a thousand years." Revelation 20:1-7 says that Christ will reign for 1,000 years after His return to Jerusalem. The millennium is the capstone of history. It will be a time when Jesus Christ will be the focus of all creation, and He will reign and rule visibly over all the world in power and great glory. It will be a wonderful time in which righteousness will cover the earth as water does the sea.

It is significant to note that within the annals of all human thought it is only in the Bible—and those influenced by biblical revelation—that we find history ending in triumph. All other approaches view the slope of history as moving from the ideal as a memory of the past to trying to restore former glory in the present. This is indeed the case because everything sinful man touches degenerates. Only the Bible teaches that the best is yet to come.

The major events of the millennium are:

- The binding of Satan (Revelation 20:1-3)
- The final restoration of Israel including
  –regeneration (Jeremiah 31:31-34)
  –regathering (Deuteronomy 30:1-10; Isaiah 11:11–12:6; Matthew 24:31)
  –possession of the land of Israel (Ezekiel 20:42-44; 36:28-38)
  –reestablishment of the Davidic throne (2 Samuel 7:11-16; 1 Chronicles 17:10-14; Jeremiah 33:17-26)
- The righteous reign of Jesus Christ (Isaiah 2:3,4; 11:2-5)
- The loosing of Satan and his final rebellion at the end of the millennium (Revelation 20:7-10)
- The great white throne Judgment and the second resurrection or judgment of unbelieving dead (Revelation 20:11-15)

The millennium will be a time in which the Adamic curse will be rolled back (except for death) and people will live for 1,000 years. Sickness and infirmity will be virtually removed; no one will live in poverty or lack food to eat. Christ, sitting on the throne of David, will ensure equity and justice for all. However, many tasks will be delegated and mediated through a hierarchy of redeemed individuals as rewards for faithfulness in this present life. The millennial kingdom will also be a time of great spiritual triumph in which national Israel will fulfill her destiny, and the Gentiles will partake of tremendous blessings through Jesus Christ and the nation of Israel. The Bible describes the millennium as a time of righteousness, obedience, holiness, truth, and a fullness of the Holy Spirit as never before experienced.

KEY EVENTS OF THE MILLENNIUM

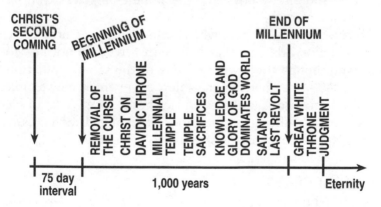

Mosaic Covenant

The Mosaic covenant (Exodus 20–23; the book of Deuteronomy), which contains the law of Moses for Israel, was given to Israel's people after they were delivered from the land of Egypt to show them how they could please God as His redeemed people. This was a *conditional* covenant given to regulate their relationship with God in the land.

The New Testament makes it very clear that the Mosaic covenant was temporary until Christ would come (Galatians 4:1-7). Many New Testament passages teach that the Mosaic law was fulfilled in Christ and now the church (a new people of God made up of believing Israel and believing Gentiles placed into one coequal body until the rapture). The church is to function under a new jurisdiction consistent with grace—the law of Christ (1 Corinthians 9:21; Galatians 6:2). Many passages teach that the law was done away with in Christ (Romans 6:14,15; 7:1-6; 1 Corinthians 9:20,21; 2 Corinthians 3:7-11; Galatians 4:1-7; 5:18; Ephesians 2–3; Hebrews 7:12; 8:6,7,13; 10:9). The law is good, but it has been fulfilled, and a new law from the same changeless God has been implemented.

During the millennium, when Israel will be restored to her land and glory, the law that will be in force will not be Mosaic even though there will be some of the same stipulations (Ezekiel 40–48). There will be a new covenant, a new temple, a new temple ritual, and a new priesthood. The writer of Hebrews says, "When the priesthood is changed, of necessity there takes place a change of law also" (Hebrews 7:12).

Mount of Olives

A mountain on the east side of the old city of Jerusalem, "Mount of Olives" is known for its olive trees. It is on this mountain, which provided the best view of the temple complex in ancient Jerusalem, that Christ gave His famous teaching on Bible prophecy that is called the Olivet Discourse (Matthew 24–25; Mark 13; Luke 17:20-37; 21:5-36). As if to punctuate the importance of the Mount of Olives to Bible prophecy, Christ ascended into heaven from this location, and two angels said, "This Jesus, who has been taken up from you into heaven, will come in just the same way as you have watched Him go into heaven" (Acts 1:11). Thus, it will be to the Mount of Olives that Jesus will descend at His second coming. Zechariah 14:4 tells us, "And in that day His feet will stand on the Mount of Olives, which is in front of Jerusalem on the east; and the Mount of Olives will be split in its middle from east to west by a very large valley, so that half of the mountain will move toward the north and the other half toward the south." The Mount of Olives is important in Bible prophecy since it will be the first place that Christ will touch upon His return.

N

Nebuchadnezzar's Dreams

In the days before sleeping pills, the Babylonian king Nebuchadnezzar had a distressing dream which, as it turns out, provided an outline of Gentile history (see Daniel 2). Daniel, a Jewish captive, was summoned to the court of the troubled king and through revelation from God repeated the king's dream to him and then interpreted it. The dream speaks of four great Gentile kingdoms that would arise successively, then eventually be crushed by a stone cut without hands. The fifth kingdom would be the final and everlasting kingdom of God who would smash the previous four Gentile kingdoms.

See also "Statue of Daniel 2."

New Covenant

The new covenant amplifies the blessing aspect of the Abrahamic covenant, especially in relationship to salvation (Jeremiah 31:31-37; Isaiah 55:3; 59:21; 61:8,9; Jeremiah 32:40; Ezekiel 16:60; 34:25-31; 37:26-28; Romans 11:25-27; Hebrews 8:7–9:1; 10:16,17). Israel, not the church, will fulfill the new covenant as prophesied in the Old Testament. The church does partake of the spiritual blessings of the Abrahamic and new covenants but does not fulfill those promises given for Israel (Romans 15:27).

There are eight main *provisions* in the new covenant:

1. The new covenant is an *unconditional* covenant involving God and both houses of Israel (Israel and Judah) (Jeremiah 31:31).
2. The new covenant is *distinct* from the Mosaic covenant (Jeremiah 31:32).

3. The new covenant promises the *regeneration* of Israel (Jeremiah 32:33; Isaiah 59:21).
4. The regeneration of Israel is to be *universal* among all Jews (Jeremiah 31:34; Isaiah 61:9; Romans 11:25-27).
5. There is a provision for the *forgiveness* of sin (Jeremiah 31:34).
6. The provision is the *indwelling* of the Holy Spirit (Jeremiah 31:33; Ezekiel 36:27).
7. Israel will be showered with material *blessings* (Jeremiah 32:41; Isaiah 61:8; Ezekiel 34:25-27).
8. The new covenant will provide for a new *sanctuary*— The Messianic or Millennial Temple (Ezekiel 37:26-28).

(From Fruchtenbaum, *Israelology,* pp. 586–87)

It should be noted that these biblical covenants contain two type of promises: physical and spiritual. The physical promises were, and still are, limited to Israel and will be fulfilled only to, in, or by Israel. Nevertheless, some of the spiritual blessings extend to the Gentiles. The blood of Jesus the Messiah is the basis of salvation (that is, "spiritual things") for all people (Jews and Gentiles), for all time (Israel, church, and millennium). The church has become a *partaker* of Jewish spiritual blessings, but the church does not *take over* the Jewish covenants. Only Israel will fulfill the new covenant as predicted throughout the Old Testament.

New Earth

In Revelation 21:1, John writes: "I saw a new heaven and a new earth; for the first heaven and the first earth passed away, and there is no longer any sea." At the end of the millennium the present creation will be destroyed so that all of the effects of Adam's fall and sin will be erased (2 Peter 3:10,12; Revelation 22:3). A new earth and heaven will then be created to remain throughout eternity. The new earth is also named the heavenly or new Jerusalem. Apparently the new earth will be one large developed city 1,500 miles high, long, and wide (Revelation 21:16). The new earth is the same as the new Jerusalem.

There is very little information given regarding the new earth. It has been said that we know far more about what won't be in the new earth than what will be. For instance, we know that, unlike the time of the millennium, there will be no sea (compare Revelation 21:1 with Psalm 72:8, Isaiah 11:9,11, Ezekiel 47:8-20 and 48:28, Zechariah 9:10 and 14:8).

New Heaven

The new heaven is spoken of in Revelation 21:1, when John writes: "I saw a new heaven and a new earth; for the first heaven and the first earth passed away, and there is no longer any sea." It will be established at the end of the millennium, and its creation is sincerely anticipated and hoped for by believers (2 Peter 3:13). Like the new earth, there is very little information recorded in the Bible about its nature; however, we do know that there will be no sun, no night (Revelation 21:23-25), and presumably no stars "because the Lord God shall illumine them" (Revelation 22:5). No doubt it will be a sight to behold. Its future existence is certain; its duration will be eternal.

New Jerusalem

God will carry forth *Jerusalem* as the name associated with His glory and presence throughout all eternity in the new Jerusalem of Revelation 3:12 and 21–22 (also Hebrews 11:8-10; 12:22-25). The eternal city will descend from heaven, continue through eternity, and be the dwelling place of the redeemed of all ages who will serve God forever (Revelation 22:3).

Jesus told His disciples in John 14:1-3 that He was going away to heaven to prepare a place for believers. Apparently the place He is constructing in heaven, at His Father's house, is the heavenly or new Jerusalem. Although built in heaven, it will also be earthly in that it is physical and geographical. It will be the earthly part of the new heavens and the new earth which will replace the current heavens and earth after their destruction. After this present earth has been destroyed by fire (2 Peter 3:10), the new city will descend from heaven (Revelation 21:1-3).

Revelation is very specific and detailed about the city, its inhabitants, and the blessedness of the eternal state. Note the following statements about the new Jerusalem from Revelation 21–22:

- "Made ready as a bride adorned for her husband" (21:2)—a picture of maximum beauty
- "The tabernacle of God is among men" (21:3)—God and redeemed mankind will dwell together in perfect fellowship
- "He shall wipe away every tear . . . no longer be any death . . . no longer be any mourning, or crying, or pain" (21:4)—the curse and *all* of its painful effects will no longer exist—we will experience perfect bliss
- "A great and high mountain" (21:10)—the city will be on a mountain, explaining why its height is also included in the dimensions
- The city will be made of the most lavish building materials such as diamonds, emeralds, and similar costly stones, and the streets will literally be paved with gold (21:18-21)—nothing but the very best

- "The city is laid out in a square" (21:16). It will be 1,500 miles wide, long, and high.
- The city will include walls and gates but not for protection since there will no longer be any threats to our security (21:24-27).
- "No need of the sun or of the moon to shine upon it" (21:23)—light will be supplied by God's glory, and there will be no night.
- "The nations shall walk by its light, and the kings of the earth" (21:24)—there will still be national entities and governing authorities.
- "River of the water of life, clear as crystal, coming from the throne of God and of the Lamb, in the middle of its street" (21:1,2)—no ocean or sea but there will be a flowing stream of water.
- "The tree of life, bearing twelve kinds of fruit, yielding its fruit every month; and the leaves of the tree were for the healing of the nations" (22:2)—we will apparently be able to eat, but not have to, and all our physical needs will be abundantly met.

John's vision leaves no doubt that citizens of this new Jerusalem, *the* eternal city, will exist in conditions unlike any this world has known. If you are a believer in Jesus Christ, then this will be your home for eternity. You have a great future in Christ.

Numbers in Prophecy

We believe that numbers relating to Bible prophecy should be taken literally—especially in Revelation—because there are no contextual factors to suggest otherwise. The only motive for nonliteralists to advocate a symbolic meaning seems to be the fact that if they took them literally it would destroy their approach to Bible prophecy. It may be that there is symbolic meaning attached to particular numbers but that doesn't mean they are not, at the same time, used to designate literal sequence. In the Bible a month is 30 days and a year is 360 days. In conjunction with numbers, we also believe that days mean days, weeks mean weeks, months mean months, and years mean years. In summary: Numbers count.

7 Years This is the length of the entire tribulation period as developed from the 70 weeks of Daniel 9:24-27. The seven years are composed of two periods of 3½ years.

42 Months This is a time reference of three-and-a-half years that is used in Revelation 11:2 and 13:5 in conjunction with the other time indicators for 3½ years [that is, 1,260 days and times (2), time (1), and half a time (½)].

75-Day Interval According to Daniel 12:11,12 mention is made of 1,290 days from the midpoint of the tribulation. An extra 30 days are added to the normal 3½ years (1,260 days). Daniel says, "How blessed is he who keeps waiting and attains to the 1,335 days!" Thus, the extra 30 days added to the 45 days comes to a total of 75 days. This will likely be the time in which the sheep-and-goat judgment of Matthew 25 takes place and perhaps additional time for setting up the millennium after the devastation of the tribulation. Nevertheless, there is an interval of 75 days between the tribulation and the millennium.

1,260 Days The 3½ years of half the tribulation are sometimes expressed by giving the total number of days that would transpire in Revelation 11:3 and 12:6. One of the benefits, whether intended or not, is that it lets us know precisely how long 3½ years and 42 months are—down to the very day.

144,000   This is a literal number and tells us how many male, Jewish virgins are sealed in their foreheads by God for special ministry during the tribulation (Revelation 7:1-8; 14:1-5). There are 12,000 from the tribe of Judah; 12,000 from the tribe of Reuben; 12,000 from the tribe of Gad; 12,000 from the tribe of Asher; 12,000 from the tribe of Naphtali; 12,000 from the tribe of Manasseh; 12,000 from the tribe of Simeon; 12,000 from the tribe of Levi; 12,000 from the tribe of Issachar; 12,000 from the tribe of Zebulun; 12,000 from the tribe of Joseph; 12,000 from the tribe of Benjamin.

Olivet Discourse

Shortly before His crucifixion, Jesus delivered a final public discourse known as the Olivet Discourse (Matthew 24–25; Mark 13; Luke 17:20-37; 21:5-36). This eschatological sermon relates to Israel's future time during the tribulation. Working from the more expansive text of Matthew 24, the discourse could be outlined as follows:

- The disciples' questions (24:3)
- Signs of the first half of the tribulation (24:4-14)
- The midpoint of the tribulation—abomination of desolation (24:15-20)
- Beginning of the second half of the tribulation—"great tribulation" (24:21,22)
- Rise of false Christs and false prophets (24:23-28)
- The second coming in glory (24:29-31)
- The fig tree illustration (24:32-35)
- The days of Noah illustration (24:36-39)
- Comparison of two men and women (24:40,41)
- The faithful householder illustration (24:42-44)
- The wise servant illustration (24:45-51)

The Olivet Discourse is given to Israel—not the church. It parallels many of the details of the tribulation as found in Revelation 6–19. This discourse doesn't include the rapture. This also does not refer to the A.D. 70 judgment that is recorded in Luke 21:20-24. Perhaps the main reason events described in the discourse are still future is due to the language of deliverance for Israel. This is not an event that has happened yet. In the A.D. 70 judgment, Israel was judged—not delivered as depicted in Matthew 24.

The Olivet Discourse and Zechariah 12–14 are parallel passages that refer to the same events. These three chapters in Zechariah include three important factors: 1) Jerusalem is surrounded by the nations who are seeking to destroy her (12:2-9; 14:2-7); 2) the Lord will fight for Israel and Jerusalem and defeat the nations who have come to lay siege against the city (14:1-8); and 3) at this same time the Lord will also save Israel from its sins and it will be converted to belief in the Messiah (12:9-14). This is what Matthew 24 talks about.

P

Palestinian Covenant

The Palestinian covenant is an expansion of the land aspect of the Abrahamic covenant. The Palestinian covenant, in essence, gives the land of Israel to the Jews (Deuteronomy 29:1–30:10). It does not mean that they will always be in the land and enjoying it, but it does mean that ultimately Israel will own and live in the land for perpetuity. Furthermore, the Palestinian covenant gives the modern state of Israel a right to the land founded in 1948.

The following are the eight provisions of the Palestinian covenant relating to the land (2–8 relate to the various facets of Israel's final *restoration*):

1. Moses prophesied Israel's coming disobedience to the Mosaic law and subsequent *scattering* over the face of the earth (29:2–30:2).
2. Israel will *repent* (30:2).
3. Messiah will *return* (30:3).
4. Israel will be *regathered* (30:3,4).
5. Israel will *possess* the promised land (30:5).
6. Israel will be *regenerated* (30:6).
7. The enemies of Israel will be *judged* (30:7).
8. Israel will receive *full blessing*, specifically the blessings of the messianic kingdom (30:8-10).

(From Fruchtenbaum, *Israelology*, p. 582)

The Palestinian covenant reaffirmed Israel's title deed to the land as originally given in the Abrahamic covenant. As an unconditional covenant, Israel's disobedience does not invalidate her ownership of the land; however, disobedience affects her enjoyment of the land. The Palestinian covenant was viewed as valid centuries later (see, for example, Ezekiel 16:1-63) and is still in force today. The following chart outlines Israel's relationship to the land.

ISRAEL AND THE LAND

ISRAEL IN THE LAND

Exodus		Postexilic		Modern Return		Millennium
1400 B.C.	586 516		A.D. 70	1948	FUTURE ➡	
	Babylonian Captivity		Diaspora		2nd half tribulation	

ISRAEL OUT OF THE LAND

Partial Rapture

This view teaches that the rapture occurs before the tribulation, but only "spiritual" Christians will be taken. Other Christians will remain to be purified through the trials of the tribulation. Some versions teach multiple raptures throughout the tribulation.

See also "Rapture."

PARTIAL RAPTURE

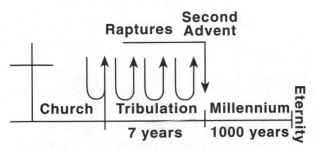

Petra

Petra is the current name of an abandoned city in southern Jordan located at Mount Seir within a basin. Petra, known in the Bible as Bozrah, will likely be the location where the Jewish remnant will flee during the middle of the tribulation. The only way in and out of the city is through a narrow passageway that extends for about a mile and is usually traveled by foot or on horseback.

See also "Bozrah."

Postmillennialism

One of the three major views of Bible prophecy (the others are amillennialism and premillennialism), postmillennialism teaches that Christ's kingdom is now being extended throughout the world through the preaching of the gospel. It states that a majority of inhabitants will be converted to Christ, resulting in a consequent Christianization of the current world's society. The English theological term is made up of the following Latin elements: *post* means "after," *mille* means "thousand," and *annus* means "years." Postmillennialism relates to the second coming of Christ to the earth—that Christ will return to earth "after the thousand years."

Postmillennialism teaches that the current age is the millennium, which is not necessarily a literal thousand years. Postmillennialists believe that through spiritual means there will be progressive growth of righteousness, prosperity, and development in every sphere of life as a growing majority of Christians eventually subdue the world for Christ. Then, after Christianity has dominated the world for a long time (the church's glorious reign of victory), Christ will return. At this time, like amillennialism, postmillennialism teaches that there will be a general resurrection, destruction of this present creation, and entry into the eternal state. Postmillennialism differs from premillennialism and amillennialism in that it optimistically believes that this victory will be realized without the need for a cataclysmic return of Christ to impose righteousness. Rather, victory will result from the faithful application of means available during our present age.

Postmillennialism did not really develop into a distinct system of eschatology until after the reformation. Prior to that time there was development of various elements that later were included in the theological mix of modern postmillennialism. Postmillennialism was the last major millennial position to develop.

John Walvoord notes that there are two principle types of postmillennialism:

> Stemming from [Daniel] Whitby [1638–1726], these groups provided two types of postmillennialism which have persisted to the twentieth century: (1) a Biblical type . . . finding its material in the Scriptures and its power in God; (2) the evolutionary or liberal theological type which bases its proof on

confidence in man to achieve progress through natural means. These two widely separated systems of belief have one thing in common, the idea of ultimate progress and solution of present difficulties (*Millennial Kingdom*, p. 27).

Postmillennialism was the dominant view of the millennium in America during much of the nineteenth century, but it virtually became extinct until the 1960s. The last years have witnessed an upsurge in postmillennialism through the Christian Reconstruction movement in some conservative arenas.

POSTMILLENNIALISM

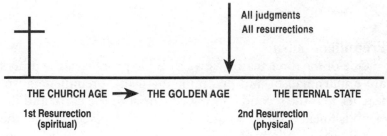

Posttribulationism

Posttribulationism teaches that all Christians will be taken in the rapture at the end of the seven-year tribulation. Of those holding this view, some do not distinguish the rapture and the second coming as separate events. Others distinguish between the rapture and second coming, believing that the rapture occurs moments before the second coming so that those raptured may return with Christ at His return to earth.

POSTTRIBULATIONAL RAPTURE

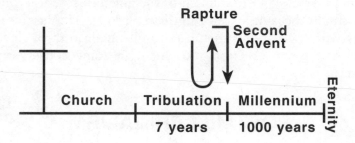

Premillennialism

One of the three major views of Bible prophecy (the others are amillennialism and postmillennialism), premillennialism teaches that the second coming of Christ to the earth and the establishment of His kingdom will take place before the 1,000-year kingdom of Revelation 20:1-7. The English theological term is made up of the following Latin elements: *pre* means "before," *mille* means "thousand," and *annus* means "years." Premillennialism means that Christ will return to earth "before the thousand years."

There are hundreds of millenium references in the Old Testament that speak of the time of Israel's end-time restoration to the land in blessing. However, it is not until John receives his revelation on Patmos that the length of Messiah's earthly reign is specified.

PREMILLENNIALISM

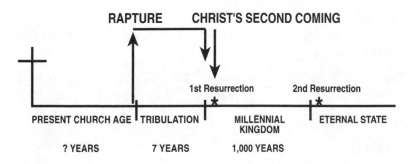

Dispensational premillennialism (the majority premillennial view) holds that there will be a future, literal, thousand-year reign of Jesus Christ upon the earth following the events of the rapture, tribulation, and second coming. There are several forms of premillennialism that differ in how the rapture relates to the tribulation, but all teach that the millennium is 1,000 literal years and follows Christ's second advent.

Premillennialism, or chiliasm as it was known in the early church, was the earliest of the three millennial systems to arise. Church historian Philip Schaff explains:

> The most striking point in the eschatology of the ante-Nicene Age is the prominent chiliasm, or millenarianism, that is the belief of a visible reign of Christ in glory on earth with the risen saints for a thousand years, before the general resurrection and judgment. It was indeed not the doctrine of the church embodied in any creed or form of devotion, but a widely current opinion of distinguished teachers (*History of the Christian Church*, vol. 2, p. 614).

Premillennialism fell out of favor during the Middle Ages but was revived by the Puritans and other Protestants in the seventeenth century. It is the viewpoint of a majority of those who are conservative in their approach to biblical interpretation.

See also "Pretribulationism," "Midtribulationism," "Post-tribulationism," "Partial Rapture," "Prewrath Rapture."

Preterism

Preterism addresses the interpretive question, "When will a prophecy be fulfilled in history?" It is one of four possible interpretive views regarding the role of timing in Bible prophecy. The four views are simple in the sense that they reflect the only possibilities in relation to time—past (preterism), present (historicism), future (futurism), and timeless (idealism).

The preterists teach that most, if not all, prophecy has already been fulfilled. They argue that major prophetic portions of Scripture (such as the Olivet Discourse and the book of Revelation) were fulfilled in events surrounding the A.D. 70 destruction of Jerusalem by the Romans. They believe they are compelled to take such a view because Matthew 24:34 and its parallel passages say that "this generation will not pass away until all these things take place." They argue that this means it had to take place in the first century. Revelation, they advocate, says something similar in the passages that say Christ is coming "quickly" or that His return is "at hand." Having settled in their minds that these prophecies had to take place in the first century, they believe they are justified in making the rest of the language fit into a local (Jerusalem), instead of a worldwide, fulfillment.

There are three kinds of preterism. For lack of better terms, we will call them mild, moderate, and extreme.

Mild preterists believe that the past fulfillment occurred during the first three centuries as God waged war on the two early enemies of the church: Israel and Rome. Israel was defeated in A.D. 70 and Rome in the fourth century.

Moderate preterists believe that almost all prophecy was fulfilled in the A.D. 70 event, but they believe that a few passages still teach a future second coming (Acts 1:9-11; 1 Corinthians 15:51-53; 1 Thessalonians 4:16,17).

Extreme preterists, or *consistent* preterists as they prefer to be known, believe that all Bible prophecy was fulfilled in the destruction of Jerusalem in A.D. 70. They believe that if there is a future second coming the Bible doesn't talk about it.

Pretribulational Rapture

This view teaches that all Christians will be taken in the rapture before the beginning of the seven-year tribulation. This rapture could happen at any moment, without warning, since no signs must precede it. The rapture is that event which ends the current church age, enabling God to finish His plan of redemption with national Israel during the tribulation. This is the perspective of the authors of this book.

Pretribulationism

First Thessalonians 4:17 teaches the fact of the rapture: "We . . . shall be *caught up* together with them . . ." (emphasis added). *Rapture,* in this verse, comes from the Latin translation of the Greek *harpazō* and is accurately rendered into English by "caught up" (NASB). A debate swirls around *when* this rapture takes place relative to the tribulation.

Like the trinity, the timing of the rapture must be developed from proper interpretation and the harmonization of many biblical passages. Therefore, pretribulationism can best

PRETRIBULATIONAL RAPTURE

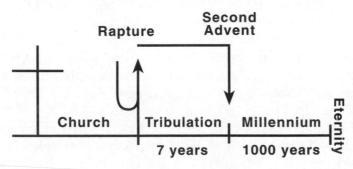

be understood by looking at the doctrine in three aspects: 1) foundational issues, 2) specific arguments from the Bible, and 3) practical implications. The doctrine of pretribulationism is depicted in the "house" diagram on the next page.

There are four foundation stones providing the biblical basis for pretribulationism: 1) consistent literal interpretation, 2) premillennialism, 3) futurism, and 4) a distinction between Israel and the church. These are not mere suppositions but rather are important biblical doctrines.

Literal Interpretation Consistent literal interpretation is essential to properly understanding what God is saying in the Bible. The dictionary defines literal as "belonging to letters." Further, it says literal interpretation involves an approach "based on the actual words in their ordinary meaning, . . . not going beyond the facts" (*Webster's New Twentieth-Century Dictionary*, unabridged, 2d ed., s.v. "literal"). "Literal interpretation of the Bible simply means to explain the original sense of the Bible according to the normal and customary usages of its language" (Paul Tan, *Interpretation*, p. 29). How is

THE PRE-TRIB RAPTURE DOCTRINE

Practical Motivation for Godly Living, Evangelism, & Missions

Pre-Trib Rapture		
• Contrasts Between Comings		
• Interval Needed Between Comings		
• Doctrine of Imminency		
• Nature of the Tribulation		
• Nature of the Church		
• Work of the Holy Spirit		
Premillen-nialism	Futurism	Israel/Church Distinction
Literal Interpretation		

this done? It can only be accomplished through the grammatical, historical, contextual methods of interpretation.

When the Bible is consistently interpreted literally, from Genesis to Revelation, then a pretribulational conclusion is hard to avoid.

Premillennialism The next biblical foundation stone supporting pretribulationism is premillennialism. Premillennialism teaches that the second advent will occur before Christ's 1,000-year reign upon earth from Jerusalem. Premillennialism is the natural conclusion of a literal interpretation of Revelation 20.

Futurism The third biblical foundation stone for pretribulationism is futurism. A literal interpretation of the Bible makes it clear that the tribulation is a future event.

Distinction Between Israel and the Church The final foundational essential is the biblical understanding that God's single program for history includes two peoples—Israel and the church. This is often known as dispensationalism. The purpose for the rapture is to end the church age so that God may return and complete His program with Israel. This would be impossible if the church and Israel are combined.

Operating consistently upon the foundation of these four biblical foundations are six specific biblical arguments for pretribulationism.

The Imminent Coming of Christ The New Testament uses many different terms in teaching that Christ could come at any moment. Some Bible teachers use the English word *imminency* to encompass the biblical teaching of this truth. Imminency means that other things *may* happen before the coming event, but nothing else *must* take place before it happens. Only pretribulationism teaches a truly imminent rapture (consistent with the New Testament), since it is the only view that doesn't require anything to happen before the rapture.

The Purpose of the Tribulation The Bible teaches that the tribulation is primarily a time of preparation for Israel's restoration (Deuteronomy 4:29,30; Jeremiah 30:4-11). While the church is told that it will experience tribulation in general during this present age (John 16:33), it is never mentioned in the Old or New Testaments as participating in Israel's time of trouble, which includes the great tribulation, the day of the Lord, and the wrath of God. Pretribulationism gives the best answer to the biblical fact that the church is never mentioned as participating in tribulational events, while references to Israel are found throughout that time.

The Nature of the Church   Only pretribulationism is able to give full biblical import to the New Testament teaching that the church differs significantly from Israel. The church is said to be a mystery (Ephesians 3) by which Jews and Gentiles are united in one body in Christ (Ephesians 2). This explains why the translation of the church is never mentioned in any passage dealing with the second coming after the tribulation and why the church is promised deliverance from the time of God's wrath during the tribulation (Revelation 3:10; 1 Thessalonians 1:9,10; 5:9). The church is promised that all believers will be taken to the Father's house in heaven (John 14:1-3), not to the earth as other views would demand.

The Work of the Holy Spirit   Since the most likely interpretation of the "restrainer of evil" in 2 Thessalonians 2 refers to the indwelling ministry of the Holy Spirit (who is at work through the body of Christ during the current church age), then this view supports pretribulationism. Since "the lawless one" (the beast or Antichrist) cannot be revealed until the restrainer is taken away, it follows that the tribulation cannot occur until the church is removed.

Contrasts Between Comings   The rapture is characterized in the New Testament as a "translation or resurrection coming" (1 Corinthians 15:51,52; 1 Thessalonians 4:15-17) in which the Lord comes *for* His church to take her to His Father's house (John 14:3). On the other hand, Christ's second advent *with* His saints (the church, Revelation 19) is when He descends from heaven and arrives on earth to stay and set up His messianic kingdom (Zechariah 14:4,5; Matthew 24:27-31). All of the differences between the two events are harmonized naturally by pretribulationism, while other views are not able to comfortably account for such differences.

An Interval Needed Between Comings   A number of items in the New Testament are best harmonized by the pretribulational time gap of at least seven years between comings. Note two examples best explained by an interval: First, an interval is needed in order for all church-age saints to appear before the judgment seat of Christ in heaven (2 Corinthians 5:10). Revelation 19:7-10 speaks of just such a judgment occurring in heaven in preparation for Christ's return to earth. Second, an interval allows for the translation of all believers on earth (pretribulational rapture) and yet has time for millions of new believers during the tribulation, who are in nonresurrection bodies at the second coming, to provide the initial population base for the millennium (Isaiah 65:20-25) and be participants in the sheep-and-goat judgment at the second advent (Matthew 25:31-46).

Dr. Renald Showers has clearly summarized the practical implications of pretribulationism:

> The fact that the glorified, holy Son of God could step through the door of heaven at any moment is intended by God to be the most pressing, incessant motivation for holy living and aggressive ministry (including missions, evangelism and Bible teaching) and the greatest cure for lethargy and apathy. It should make a major difference in every Christian's values, actions, priorities and goals" (*Maranatha,* p. 256).

Prewrath Rapture

This view, developed in the 1970s, teaches that all Christians will be taken in the rapture approximately three-fourths of the way through the tribulation. It further teaches that Christ's second coming will commence before the outpouring of the seven bowl judgments of Revelation 16.

PREWRATH RAPTURE

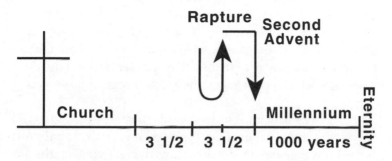

Pseudo-Ephraem

As a historical source, Pseudo-Ephraem is a reference to an apocalyptic sermon containing two proto-rapture statements that date from the fourth to seventh centuries A.D. Known today as "Sermon on the End of the World," with extant copies in Greek and Latin, the sermon claims the authorship of the Syrian church father Ephraem of Nisibis (306–373), the most important and prolific of the Syrian fathers and a witness to Christianity on the fringes of the Roman empire. While there is little support for Ephraem as the actual author of the "Sermon on the End of the World," Pseudo-Ephraem was greatly influenced by Ephraem's writings.

The exact date of the original sermon is uncertain, with suggested dates ranging from as early as A.D. 373 to as late as 565–627. While a late date (seventh century) seems to have the consensus of support, any reasonable date is acceptable in relation to the history of the rapture and premillennialism. Some of the most significant words in the sermon are the sentences:

Why therefore do we not reject every care of earthly actions and prepare ourselves for the meeting of the Lord Christ, so that he may draw us from the confusion, which overwhelms all the world? . . . All the saints and elect of God are gathered together before the tribulation, which is to come, and are taken to the Lord, in order that they may not see at any time the confusion which overwhelms the world because of our sins.

These words proclaim a divine act of mercy and intervention enacted upon believers prior to a time of great calamity. Pseudo-Ephraem believed Christians were living in the last days and would soon experience a gathering or rapture of believers prior to a 42-month period of tribulation in which the Antichrist would reign. These months would culminate in the return of Christ, final judgment, and the eternal punishment of the Antichrist and Satan.

The sermon is unlike most Byzantine accounts which have some shortening of the time intervals by God during the rule of the Antichrist. Instead, Pseudo-Ephraem has Christians being removed from the time of tribulation, even though it is a 3½-year tribulation (instead of 7-year one).

The proto-rapture statements and chronology are very clear, although there are obvious shortcomings in some of its particulars from the contemporary pretribulational perspective. What is most important for contemporary readers, however, are not the differences but the similarities of its perspective with pretribulationism. The sermon proclaimed expectation of the removal of Christians from the earth prior to a specific period of tribulation—and it did so more than 1200 years ago.

R

Rapture

Some critics have noted that the word *rapture* is never used in the Bible. While this is true of most English versions, Latin translators of the Greek New Testament *did* use the word *rapere*, which is the root of the English term *rapture*. Many contemporary theological terms have been derived from a Latin base. Throughout much of the history of the Western church, Latin was the accepted language of theological discussion. As a result, many theological terms developed out of this language (for instance, trinity, millennium, imminence). *Rapture* is also such a word. There are many terms used in the New Testament to refer to the rapture event. To claim that the rapture should be dismissed on the grounds of language is naively incorrect.

The teaching of the rapture is most clearly presented in 1 Thessalonians 4:13-18. In this passage Paul informs his readers that living Christians at the time of the rapture will be reunited with those who have died in Christ before them. In verse 17 the English phrase "caught up" translates from the Greek word *harpazó*, which means "to seize upon with force" or "to snatch up." This word is used 14 times in the Greek New Testament in a variety of ways.

Sometimes the New Testament uses *harpazó* with the sense of "stealing," "carrying off," or "dragging away" (Matthew 12:29; John 10:12). It also can have the meaning of "to lead away forcibly" (John 6:15; 10:28,29; Acts 23:10; Jude 23). However, for our purposes, a third usage is significant. This usage is that of God's Spirit carrying someone away. We see this usage illustrated in Acts 8:39 where Philip, upon completion of the baptism of the Ethiopian eunuch, is raptured or "caught up" and divinely transported from the desert to the coastal town of Azotus (see also 2 Corinthians 12:2,4; 1 Thessalonians 4:17; Revelation 12:5). Similarly, the church will, in a moment of time, be taken from earth to heaven. It is not surprising that contemporary author Hal Lindsey has called this unique event "The Great Snatch."

There are a multitude of theories as to when the rapture will take place in relation to the tribulation among premillennialists. We believe "the Great Snatch" will occur before the 7 year tribulation.

See also "Pretribulationism," "Partial Rapture," "Midtribulationism," "Prewrath," "Posttribulationism."

Red Horse Judgment
See "Four Horsemen."

Remnant
Throughout Israel's history there has been a perpetual strand of righteous, believing men and women, who have been in proper relationship with God and maintained the human portion of God's unconditional covenants with His people. In the present age, all Jews who are saved are placed into the body of Christ. Yet, according to Romans 11:25-27, the present spiritual blindness of Israel is only temporary and Israel will be restored to a full and vital relationship after the second coming of Christ. Throughout the present age and the tribulation there will be Jews who come to a saving knowledge of Jesus Christ. Among these will be the 144,000 Jewish "bond-servants" spoken of in Revelation 7:1-4 and 14:4.

Both Israel and Jerusalem will have a very special role in the millennium, which will be the occasion for the final physical and spiritual restoration of Israel. This restoration is described in Ezekiel 37 and is summarized in verses 21,22:

And say to them, "Thus says the Lord GOD, 'Behold, I will take the sons of Israel from among the nations where they have gone, and I will gather them from every side and bring them into their own land; and I will make them one nation in the land, on the mountains of Israel; and one king will be king for all of them; and they will no longer be two nations, and they will no longer be divided into two kingdoms.' "

The restoration of Israel will include regeneration, regathering, possession of "the land," and reestablishment of the Davidic throne. There are also several other features of the restoration that will accompany the events listed above. According to Jeremiah 3:18 and Ezekiel 37:15-23, the nation will be reunited so that its previous twofold division of Israel and Judah will be eliminated. As a nation, it will become the center of Gentile attention (Isaiah 14:1,2; 49:22,23; Zephaniah 3:20; Zechariah 8:23), and it will enjoy all of the physical and spiritual conditions noted throughout Scripture by the prophets (Isaiah 32:16-20; 35:5-10; 51:3; 55:12,13; 61:10,11).

Restrainer

Second Thessalonians 2:1-12 discusses a "man of lawlessness" being held back or restrained (2:6,7) until a later time. This man of lawlessness is the Antichrist who will arise during the tribulation. Interpreting the restrainer of evil (2:6) as the indwelling ministry of the Holy Spirit at work through the body of Christ during the current age makes the best sense of the biblical text and supports the pretribulational interpretation of the future. Since "the lawless one" (the beast or Antichrist) cannot be revealed until the "restrainer" (the Holy Spirit) is taken away (2:7,8), the tribulation cannot occur until the church is removed.

The key to the above scenario is whether the Holy Spirit is the restrainer. While this is not the only interpretation, it fits grammatically and theologically. At the rapture of the church, the special presence of the Spirit as the indweller of believers will terminate as abruptly as it began at Pentecost. Once the body of Christ has been caught away or raptured to heaven, the Holy Spirit's ministry will revert back to what He did for believers during the Old Testament era. His function of restraining evil through the body of Christ (John 16:7-11; 1 John 4:4) will cease. Once this happens, literally "all hell will break loose" as the Antichrist arises and the tribulation begins.

Resurrections, Order of

The concept of future bodily resurrection is found throughout the Bible. These resurrections fall into two categories: the first resurrection or the resurrection of life and the second resurrection or the resurrection of judgment (John 5:28,29).

The first resurrection includes the redeemed of all the ages. The timing of the resurrection of these individuals depends upon whether they were Old Testament saints, Christians living before or at the time of the rapture, or Christian martyrs of the tribulation. All of these comprise the category "resurrection of life."

The second category, the "resurrection of judgment," includes the unredeemed of all the ages, who will be raised at the end of the millennium, judged before the great white throne, and cast into the lake of fire.

The resurrections do not occur at the same time and sequentially are as follows:

1. The resurrection of Jesus Christ as the first fruit of many to be raised (Romans 6:9; 1 Corinthians 15:23; Colossians 1:18; Revelation 1:18)

2. The resurrection of the redeemed at Christ's coming (Daniel 12:2; Luke 14:14; John 5:29; 1 Thessalonians 4:16; Revelation 20:4,6)

a) Resurrection of the church at the rapture
b) Resurrection of Old Testament believers at the second coming (Jews and Gentiles)
c) Resurrection of all martyred tribulation saints at the second coming (Jews and Gentiles)
d) Resurrection of all millennial believers after the millennium

3. The resurrection of the unredeemed (Revelation 20: 11-14).

THE COMING JUDGMENTS AND RESURRECTIONS

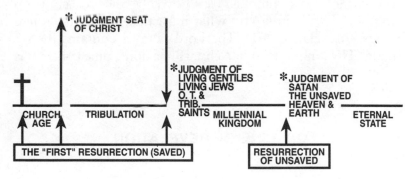

Revelation, Book of

The book of Revelation is the most extensive section of the Bible that deals with end-time prophecy. John's vision was recorded late in the first century, while he was a prisoner for political and religious reasons on the Island of Patmos. As a young man, John had been an eyewitness of the life and ministry of Jesus Christ. Now, in his old age, he is given a vision of the future from the same Lord.

In John's revelation, history is divided into three epochs. According to Revelation 1:19, John was instructed to "write therefore *the things which you have seen*, and *the things which are*, and *the things which shall take place after these things*" (emphasis added).

Most of Revelation (chapters 4–19) is spent detailing the chronological progression of the seven-year tribulation. But there are periodic pauses in sequence to introduce key figures and alternate between the heavenly (God's) perspective and the earthly (human) perspective. It is important to note that the section on the tribulation begins with the heavenly perspective. As we move from Revelation 2–3 (representative of the present church age) to Revelation 4–19 (the tribulation section), John is summoned by a heavenly voice to "come up here, and I will show you what must take place after these things" (Revelation 4:1). The Lord's Prayer contains the request "Thy kingdom come. Thy will be done, on earth as it is

OUTLINE OF REVELATION

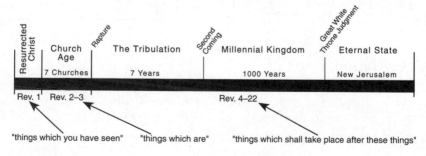

in heaven" (Matthew 6:10). Revelation 4–5 is the beginning of the seven-year period that inaugurates the answer to this request. Chapter 4 introduces us to the heavenly drama of the need for someone who is worthy to execute God's mandate. Chapter 5 shows us that Jesus Christ is the only one capable of taking the title-deed of earth and executing its mandate.

Many of the judgments in Revelation relate to three specific divisions: seals, trumpets, and bowls. The descriptions of these categories seem to show that: 1) the seals represent the beginning of judgment, 2) the trumpets represent the continuation of judgment, and 3) the bowls represent the climax of God's judgment. (See also "Seals," "Trumpets," and "Bowls.")

Chapter 7 returns us to the heavenly perspective in which there is a temporary suspension of the judgments. Verses 2-8 speak of the sealing of the 144,000 Jewish evangelists, and verses 9-17 describe the salvation of Gentiles (of many nationalities).

The second series of judgments are identified as trumpet judgments, perhaps because they are implemented through angels. These are recorded in Revelation 8–9.

These chapters return to the heavenly perspective and cover a time of preparation in which there is a long pause in John's presentation of the campaign of heaven against earth. In chapter 10, a small, opened scroll, held by an angel, contains seven thunders—apparently a revelation about the mystery of God that will finally be revealed in relation to Christ's second coming. This announcement is viewed as bittersweet (verse 9). Initially it is sweet to know of the Lord's glorious return, but the judgments that accompany His return will be a bitter experience for many.

In the middle of John's vision, many personalities and descriptions of their roles in the tribulation are presented

HEAVENLY/EARTHLY CYCLE IN REVELATION
Revelation 4–20

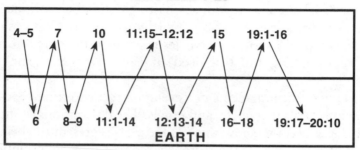

(11–15). The introduction of these key players prepares the reader of Revelation for the all-important second half of the tribulation, known as "the great tribulation."

In Revelation 16, John reveals the most severe judgments of all—the bowl judgments. These are preparations for the second coming of Christ.

The Judgment of Babylon takes place in chapters 17–18:

> "Come here, I shall show you the judgment of the great harlot."... I saw a woman sitting on a scarlet beast, full of blasphemous names, having seven heads and ten horns. And the woman was clothed in purple and scarlet, and adorned with gold and precious stones and pearls... and upon her forehead a name was written, a mystery, "BABLYON THE GREAT, THE MOTHER OF HARLOTS AND OF THE ABOMINATIONS OF THE EARTH" (Revelation 17:1,3-5).

Why does the book of Revelation devote two chapters to a description and judgment of Babylon? Babylon expert Dr. Charles Dyer tells us,

From Genesis to Revelation, Babylon occupies a prominent place in the Bible. Babylon epitomizes humanity's pride and rebellion against God. The name comes from the description of the tower around which the city was first built—*bab* (gate), *el* (god). Babel was humanity's self-appointed gateway to God, the place where they hoped to reach God by their efforts apart from His intended plan.

Babylon retained its essential nature throughout the Bible. The height of Babylon's opposition to God came when the army of Babylon destroyed Jerusalem and dismantled God's kingdom on earth. They deposed the king from the line of David and dragged him off in chains. They burned the temple of Solomon and carried off the people of Judah. Daniel described Babylon as the "head of gold" in the "times of the Gentiles"—that time when Gentile powers would rule over God's people.

But the God who predicted the triumph of Babylon also promised its ultimate destruction (*World News*, p. 141).

God is going to judge Babylon because of its supreme legacy as the opponent of God's people and program. The "times of the Gentiles" begins with Babylon and ends with its judgment. Babylon is the repository of satanic and human opposition to God and His program.

The tribulation finally comes to an end in Revelation 19. Christ's return to earth is preceded by heavenly activity. His bride, the church, has been in heaven throughout the tribulation and has made itself ready to return with Him. Revelation 19:11-13,15,16 describes Christ's demeanor as He readies for His return:

Behold, a white horse, and He who sat upon it is called Faithful and True; and in righteousness He judges and wages war. And His eyes are a flame of fire, and upon His head are many diadems; and He has a name written upon Him which no one knows except Himself. And He is clothed with a robe dipped in blood; and His name is called The Word of God. . . . And from His mouth comes a sharp sword, so that with it He may smite the nations; and He will rule them with a rod of iron; and He treads the wine press of the fierce wrath of God, the Almighty. And on His robe and on His thigh He has a name written, "KING OF KINGS, AND LORD OF LORDS."

At the second coming, Christ's first act is the destruction of His enemies.

With Antichrist's reign of terror over and judgment complete, the stage has been set for Christ's thousand-year reign. In Revelation 20, the brilliance of the millennial rule of Christ provides a stark contrast to the darkness of the tribulation.

The final chapters of Revelation (21–22) tell us wonderful details about eternity in the new heavens and new earth. Believers have a wonderful future ahead of them for all eternity, while those rejecting Christ have only the lake of fire awaiting them.

The book of Revelation provides a fitting capstone to God's Word. Taking the whole of Scripture, we have seen that what started in an undeveloped garden with two people progresses to a beautifully developed eternal city.

Revived Roman Empire

One of the core elements of end-time prophecy relating to the tribulation is the biblical prediction that there will be a revived form of the fourth of the four Gentile kingdoms predicted in Daniel 2 and 7. Since Rome was clearly the fourth kingdom, it follows that some form of that kingdom will be revived. What all the king's horses and all the king's men could not do, God will allow the Antichrist to accomplish for a brief period of time (in the future).

Daniel 7 and Revelation 13 and 17 note that a ten-nation confederacy will be revived during the tribulation period. This alliance will facilitate the world domination of the Antichrist. Dr. John Walvoord explains:

> The prediction that there will be a ten-kingdom stage of the revival of the Roman Empire is one of the important descriptive prophecies of the end time. This prophecy anticipates that there will be ten countries originally related to the Roman Empire that will constitute the Roman Empire in its revived form. . . . The prediction requires a political union and then a dictator over the ten countries (*Major Bible Prophecies*, pp. 314–15).

Developments in our own day relating to the renunification of Europe are an indication that God is preparing the world for just such a configuration as predicted thousands of years ago in the Bible.

Rewards

The church age is often a time of deferred blessing in the sense that believers of this age are promised rewards in the life to come. As believers in Christ, we are already blessed "with every spiritual blessing in the heavenly places in Christ" (Ephesians 1:3). However, the Lord promises future rewards and crowns to those who are faithful in this life and live in accordance with Christ's provision.

Rewards differ from salvation. Works do not add to or take away from one's salvation in Christ since that is not the basis on which anything is accomplished. Salvation is the result of the work *of Christ* that we trust. However, after we have placed our trust in Christ and have received the forgiveness of our sins (justification), God's plan is that we live a life of good works that bring glory to Him (Ephesians 2:10). If we are faithful to God, He will give us rewards after the rapture, at the bema or judgment seat of Christ (1 Corinthians 3:12-15; 2 Corinthians 5:10; Romans 14:10).

These rewards are pictured in Revelation 19:7-16 as the clothing the church (the bride of Christ) will wear when it descends with Christ at His second advent (19:14). These clothes are called "fine linen" because they are "the righteous acts of the saints" (19:8). Since the church in heaven is viewed as a complete entity (which it must be in order to go through the reward process and return with Christ at the second coming), it makes sense that it has been raptured before

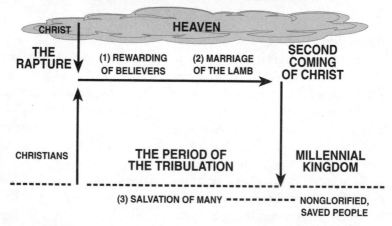

EVENTS BETWEEN THE RAPTURE AND SECOND COMING

the tribulation and undergone the evaluation for rewards during this time.

Rewards are motivations for believers in this life to remain faithful to Christ until death or the rapture. This is why Paul said, "I buffet my body and make it my slave, lest possibly, after I have preached to others, I myself should be disqualified" (1 Corinthians 9:27).

See also "Crown."

Russia

According to Ezekiel 38–39, combined forces from the south and north of Israel will launch a massive assault against Israel some time during the tribulation. Part of these forces, led by a person with the name or title of Gog, will come from territory that, today, is identified as Russia and the Commonwealth of Independent States (Ezekiel 38:2,3). Joining these northern forces will also be coalition forces from northern Africa, Turkey, and Iran (Ezekiel 38:5,6). Israel will be attacked during a time of real (or perceived) peace and security. It is only through the direct intervention of God that Israel's enemies will be defeated.

See also "Gog" and "Magog."

S

Sacrifices, Millennial

One aspect of the millennial temple described in Ezekiel 40–46, especially 43:13-27, which has given many prophecy students pause for reflection is that of the purpose and role of future sacrifices. At least four other Old Testament prophets join Ezekiel in affirming a sacrificial system at that time (Isaiah 56:7; 66:20-23; Jeremiah 33:18; Zechariah 14:16-21; Malachi 3:3,4). Such a strong and clear Scriptural testimony is enough to establish that there will be sacrifices performed in the millennial temple. But what is their purpose?

The millennial temple will be the fourth and final temple in Israel's history. It will be the central focus for worshiping Jesus Christ during the millennium. It will exist in Jerusalem throughout the 1000-year reign of Christ and will bear witness that God always intended that His chosen people, Israel, serve as a priestly nation to the other nations of the world. In the millennial temple, all that was prescribed and initiated in the Old Testament ceremonial and ritual activities will come to its fullest meaning and completion.

Acceptance of the literal interpretation of a millennial sacrificial system does not contradict New Testament passages (such as Hebrews 7:26,27 and 9:26, which teach that Jesus Christ was the perfect and final sacrifice for sin). Premillennial scholars have fully recognized the issues at hand. They offer at least two legitimate solutions to this concern. First, the sacrifices may function as a memorial to the work of Christ. This view does not, however, completely resolve all the concerns. Ezekiel says that the sacrifices are *for atonement* rather than a memorial (Ezekiel 45:15,17,20). Therefore, a second solution to the question of "why" is that the sacrifices are for ceremonial purification. Since all the sacrifices of

S

Ezekiel relate to purification of the priests for temple service, they do not depict or represent Christ's atoning sacrifice. The sacrifices of the millennial temple will not be a return to the Mosaic law, since the law has forever been fulfilled and discontinued through Christ (Romans 6:14; 7:1-6; 1 Corinthians 9:20,21; 2 Corinthians 3:7-11; Galatians 4:1-7; 5:18; Hebrews 8:13; 10:1-14).

The presence and purpose of sacrifices neither diminishes the work of Christ nor violates the normal and literal interpretation of the prophetic passages. Although there will be sacrifices, the focus of all worship will remain on the person and work of the Savior.

Satan

"Satan" means "adversary," and it effectively reflects his perpetual opposition to the plan of God. Satan is a created spirit being. He is not eternal, self-existent, omniscient, omnipresent, or omnipotent. Although he is very powerful, he is not an entity that is equal to God. The exact time of his creation is not specified in the Bible although, before his fall, he was highly privileged and powerful in heaven. There are a variety of names and images used to refer to him that portray the broad attack and deception he casts upon people, for example: "angel of light" (2 Corinthians 11:14) and "great red dragon" (Revelation 12:3). The animosity between Satan and Jesus Christ was first predicted after the sin of Adam and Eve in the Garden of Eden: "And I will put enmity between you and the woman, and between your seed and her seed; He shall bruise you on the head, and you shall bruise him on the heel" (Genesis 3:15). This conflict will continue until the end of the millennium, when Satan is judged and cast into the lake of fire.

Throughout history Satan has used deception and the offer of a counterfeit program to entice people away from God and His plan. This began in Genesis 3:5, when Satan enticed Eve, and will culminate in the tribulation and the counterfeit kingdom he offers through the Antichrist. Satan deceives people and nations. Dr. Charles Ryrie writes:

> The ultimate counterfeit will be the coming Antichrist whose activities will be in accord with Satan and who will pawn off on mankind "the lie" (2 Thessalonians 2:9 NIV). His principle activity in this arena [in relation to the nations] is to deceive the nations (Revelation 20:3). Deceive them how? Apparently into thinking they can govern righteously and bring peace in the world apart from the presence and rule of Christ (*Basic Theology*, p. 148).

During the tribulation much of Satan's work will be accomplished through the activities of the Antichrist. According to Revelation 12:7-12, at the midpoint of the tribulation Satan will be cast out of his abode in the atmospheric heavens and thrown down to earth.

> In the middle of the tribulation while war breaks out on earth between the Antichrist and the ten kings, war also breaks out in the atmospheric heavens. . . . The conflict is between the Archangel Michael and his forces and the archenemy Satan and his forces. Michael is victorious, and Satan and his cohorts are cast out of the atmospheric heavens and confined to the earth. . . .
> Satan's confinement to the earth brings two results: *First,* Satan's access to heaven is removed and he will no longer be able to stand before the Throne of God and be the accuser of the brethren. For this there is rejoicing in heaven (verses

10-12a). *Secondly*, Satan is now full of wrath (verse 12b). His anger is due to the fact that he knows his time is short, namely three and a half years. Because of Satan's wrath, it is *woe for the earth*. This is a very important point to note in the understanding of what is happening during the middle and second half of the tribulation (Fruchtenbaum, *Footsteps of the Messiah*, p. 166).

The relationship between the expulsion of Satan and the last half of the tribulation, or great tribulation, is very important because it is at this point that the true character and intent of the Antichrist is revealed in the abomination of desolation. Also at this time, the intense persecution of the Jews begins. All of this activity climaxes in the campaign of Armageddon, the defeat of the forces of Satan and the Antichrist, and the second coming of Jesus Christ. At the end of the tribulation, Satan will be bound so that he will not be active during the millennium and reign of Christ.

At the end of the thousand-year reign of Christ on earth, there will be one final rebellion by Satan and his minions. Just as prophesied in Revelation 20, Satan will be loosed at the end of the millennium and will rebel against the millennial reign of Christ. In one final grasp for power and human allegiance, Satan will manifest his true nature (as he has done throughout history) and attempt to seize the throne of God. Dr. Walvoord writes of this attempted *coup d' état:*

> The thousand years of confinement will not change Satan's nature, and he will attempt to take the place of God and receive the worship and obedience that is due God alone. He will find a ready response on the part of those who have made a profession of following Christ in the Millennium but who now show their true colors. They will surround Jerusalem in

an attempt to capture the capital city of the kingdom of David as well as of the entire world. The Scriptures report briefly, "But fire came down from heaven and devoured them" (Walvoord, *Major Bible Prophecies,* p. 404).

According to Revelation 20:10, Satan's termination will be swift but everlasting. He will be cast into the lake of fire, joining the Antichrist and the False Prophet (the Antichrist's lieutenant) (Revelation 13:11-18). The fact that the Antichrist and False Prophet are placed in the lake of fire at the second coming, prior to the millennium, demonstrates that they are finished in history. The lake of fire is the final form of hell from which no one, once placed there, ever leaves. This is why Satan is bound in the bottomless pit at the start of the millennium—because he will make one more appearance upon history's stage before he is once and for all consigned to his fate.

It seems somewhat strange that Satan, once bound, would be loosed again to rebel. Yet this activity provides to all of the created order the supreme illustration of sin and its consequences. Satan will not change and some humans, even when in a pristine environment, will manifest the sin nature acquired at the fall in the Garden of Eden (Genesis 3).

History does not merely include the human dimension of creation, it also involves the angelic as well. In a classic demonstration of interplay between the satanic and human, Satan makes his encore upon the stage of history by giving fallen humanity what it lacked during the millennium. One last time, Satan serves to embolden rebellious humanity into a deceived mob who, amazingly, thinks it can prevail in a confrontation against an omnipotent God. Finally, through the agency of a recently released Satan, all unbelievers show their chosen allegiance and are, along with Satan, swiftly and finally defeated. Then Satan is judged, followed by the judgment of the unbelieving dead, known as the great white throne judgment (Revelation 20:11-15).

Seals

The first of the three series of seven judgments that take place during the tribulation is known as seal judgments (Revelation 6; 8:1). In the ancient world, seals were used to close up a scroll of writing. Hot wax was dripped on the papyrus, then the sender's signet ring was pressed into the wax to form a mark. This mark showed that the message had not been opened before it reached the individual to whom it was sent. A thorough study of Revelation 5 indicates that the scroll that was sealed is apparently the title-deed of ownership to planet Earth. Only Jesus Christ—the Lamb of God—is found worthy to open the seal and commence the judgments of the tribulation.

First Seal (Revelation 6:1,2) The first seal is also called the white horse judgment. This first judgment is what, today, we would call a "cold war." The interpretation of this rider is hotly debated between two major views: that it represents Christ or that it represents the Antichrist. Even though in Revelation 19:11 Christ returns on a white horse, it does not mean that Christ is pictured in 6:1,2. The second view is more likely since one who comes riding a white horse usually depicts a military leader. It is the Antichrist who comes to conquer at the beginning of the tribulation, which this judgment denotes, and Christ who conquers the Antichrist at the end of the tribulation in Revelation 19.

Second Seal (Revelation 6:3,4) The second seal is the red horse judgment. The color of the horse appears to indicate blood and death since the passage says that "it was granted to take peace from the earth, and that men should slay one another; and a great sword was given to him" (verse 4). This the rider does through open warfare. Here we have one of the few instances in the tribulation when God instigates His judgment by pitting man against man.

Third Seal (Revelation 6:5,6) The black horse judgment is the third seal. The rider comes forth displaying "a pair of scales in his hand" and saying, "A quart of wheat for a denarius, and three quarts of barley for a denarius; and do not harm the oil and the wine." A severe shortage of food is indicated, which often is the case following military conflicts as mentioned in the two previous seals. The monetary description indicates that normal purchasing power will be reduced to one-eighth.

Fourth Seal (Revelation 6:7,8) The fourth seal is also called the ashen horse judgment. This is the most severe of the four judgments: "And authority was given to . . . over a fourth of the earth, to kill with sword and with famine and with pestilence and by the wild beasts of the earth."

Fifth Seal (Revelation 6:9-11) The fifth seal judgment is one that never really takes place. When the seal is broken it results in the martyrs of the tribulation crying out to God for revenge upon those unbelievers who killed them on earth. They are told that the time for vengeance has not yet come . . . but it will. The passage also expects more martyrs for Christ to join those already in heaven. Their prayer of vengeance is finally answered in Revelation 16:4-7 during the third bowl judgment.

Sixth Seal (Revelation 6:12-17) The sixth seal judgment is very severe. Six things happen: 1) a great earthquake; 2) the sun is blacked out; 3) the moon becomes like blood; 4) the stars fall to the earth; 5) the sky tears apart like a scroll; and 6) every mountain and island are moved out of their places. Rather than such events leading to repentance and prayer to God for deliverance, they lead to further rebellion against God. The people pray to the rocks and mountains to "fall on us and hide us from the presence of Him who sits on the throne, and from the wrath of the Lamb."

Seventh Seal (Revelation 8:1) The seventh seal judgment is the next series of seven judgments known as the trumpet judgments.

SEAL JUDGMENTS

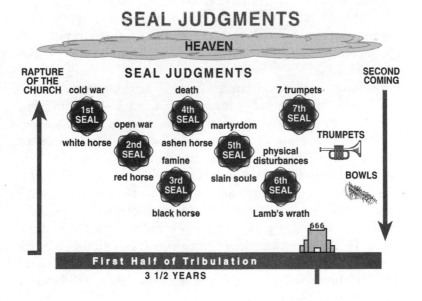

Second Coming of Christ

One of the major events in the Bible is the second coming of Jesus Christ to the earth. Jesus Christ is coming again to vanquish His enemies and to reign in righteousness upon this earth for 1,000 years. The second coming will end the tribulation and begin the millennium.

The specific setting for Christ's second advent will be related to the campaign of Armageddon. Christ will have gathered the armies of the world to Israel through the sixth bowl judgment (Revelation 16:12-16). Next, Christ will judge and destroy Babylon in one hour as the whole earth mourns (Revelation 18:10). The Antichrist will then send his armies to surround and attack Jerusalem (Zechariah 12:1-9; 14:1,2). He will also send his forces to Bozrah (Petra) in southern Jordan, the refuge of many of the Jews who fled persecution from the middle of the tribulation on (Jeremiah 49:13,14; Micah 2:12). These events will then trigger the national regeneration and conversion of Israel three days before the second coming (Hosea 6:1-3; Zechariah 12:10-14; Romans 11:25-27).

Because of these circumstances, a now-converted Israel will plead for Messiah—Jesus of Nazerath—to come and rescue them from the impossible situation of Armageddon. The second coming of Christ is, in essence, a rescue event. This is when Christ returns to the earth to defeat the Antichrist and to judge all the world's unbelievers. He will also finally deliver Israel. Christ returns first to Bozrah and rescues Israel from the Antichrist and his armies (Isaiah 14:3-21; Jeremiah 49:20-22; Joel 3:12,13; Zechariah 14:12-15; Revelation 14:19,20). After this, Christ makes His victory descent to the Mount of Olives in Jerusalem (Joel 3:14-17; Zechariah 14:3-5; Matthew 24:29,30). The second coming will be completed at that point.

There are many terms used in the New Testament that speak of Christ's coming. Most are used to refer to both the second coming and the rapture, even though they are seperate events. A study of the context determines which event the given writer has in mind.

- *harpazó*—"caught up," "to seize upon with force," "to snatch up"

  "Then we who are alive and remain shall be *caught up* together with them in the clouds to meet the Lord in the air, and thus we shall always be with the Lord" (1 Thessalonians 4:17, emphasis added).

- *episunagógé* —"gathering together," "assembly"

  "Now we request you, brethren, with regard to the coming of our Lord Jesus Christ, and our *gathering together* to Him" (2 Thessalonians 2:1, emphasis added).

- *allassó*—"to change," "to transform," "to exchange"

  "Behold, I tell you a mystery; we shall not all sleep, but we shall all be *changed*, in a moment, in the twinkling of an eye, at the last trumpet; for the trumpet will sound, and the dead will be raised imperishable, and we shall be *changed*" (1 Corinthians 15:51,52, emphasis added).

- *paralambanó*—"to take to," "to receive to oneself"

  "If I go and prepare a place for you, I will come again, and *receive* you to Myself; that where I am, there you may be also" (John 14:3, emphasis added).

- *epiphaneia*—"a manifestation," "an appearance"

  ". . . looking for the blessed hope and the *appearing* of the glory of our great God and Savior, Christ Jesus" (Titus 2:13, emphasis added).

- *rhuomai*—"to draw to oneself," "to rescue," "to deliver"

  "... and to wait for His Son from heaven, whom He raised from the dead, that is Jesus, who *delivers* us from the wrath to come" (1 Thessalonians 1:10, emphasis added).

- *apokalupsis*—"an uncovering," "laying bare," "a revealing, revelation"

  "Therefore, gird your minds for action, keep sober in spirit, fix your hope completely on the grace to be brought to you at the *revelation* of Jesus Christ" (1 Peter 1:13, emphasis added).

RAPTURE & SECOND COMING PASSAGES

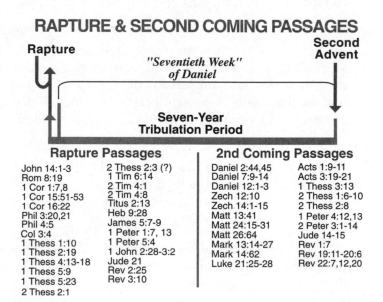

Rapture Passages		2nd Coming Passages	
John 14:1-3	2 Thess 2:3 (?)	Daniel 2:44,45	Acts 1:9-11
Rom 8:19	1 Tim 6:14	Daniel 7:9-14	Acts 3:19-21
1 Cor 1:7,8	2 Tim 4:1	Daniel 12:1-3	1 Thess 3:13
1 Cor 15:51-53	2 Tim 4:8	Zech 12:10	2 Thess 1:6-10
1 Cor 16:22	Titus 2:13	Zech 14:1-15	2 Thess 2:8
Phil 3:20,21	Heb 9:28	Matt 13:41	1 Peter 4:12,13
Phil 4:5	James 5:7-9	Matt 24:15-31	2 Peter 3:1-14
Col 3:4	1 Peter 1:7, 13	Matt 26:64	Jude 14-15
1 Thess 1:10	1 Peter 5:4	Mark 13:14-27	Rev 1:7
1 Thess 2:19	1 John 2:28-3:2	Mark 14:62	Rev 19:11-20:6
1 Thess 4:13-18	Jude 21	Luke 21:25-28	Rev 22:7,12,20
1 Thess 5:9	Rev 2:25		
1 Thess 5:23	Rev 3:10		
2 Thess 2:1			

• *parousia*—"a being present, presence," "a coming," "an arrival"

"Be patient, therefore, brethren, until the *coming* of the Lord. Behold, the farmer waits for the precious produce of the soil, being patient about it, until it gets the early and late rains. You too be patient; strengthen your hearts, for the *coming* of the Lord is at hand" (James 5:7,8, emphasis added).

It is important to note the difference between the second coming and the earlier event of the rapture of the church. Note the following passages that distinguish the two events:

Based upon a comparison of these passages, note the differences in the character of the two events:

RAPTURE/2ND COMING CONTRASTS

Rapture/Translation	Second Coming Established Kingdom
1. Translation of all believers	1. No translation at all
2. Translated saints go to heaven	2. Translated saints return to earth
3. Earth not judged	3. Earth judged and righteousness established
4. Imminent, any-moment, signless	4. Follows definite predicted signs, including tribulation
5. Not in the Old Testament	5. Predicted often in Old Testament
6. Belivers only	6. Affects all humanity
7. Before the day of wrath	7. Concluding the day of wrath
8. No reference to Satan	8. Satan bound
9. Christ comes *for* His own	9. Christ comes *with* His own
10. He comes in the *air*	10. He comes to the *earth*
11. He claims His bride	11. He comes with His bride
12. Only His own see Him	12. Every eye shall see Him
13. Tribulation begins	13. Millennial Kingdom begins

Sermon on the Mount

Early in His ministry Christ gave a discourse popularly known as the "Sermon on the Mount" (Matthew 5–7; Luke 6:17-49). This "sermon" does not present a way of salvation but outlines the righteous standard needed for a citizen of the Lord's kingdom. It is contrasted with the popular notions of the Scribes and Pharisees, who usually were at odds with Christ's teachings. Christ presents an impossible standard for a fallen human, whether Jew or Gentile, to live up to. Christ declares, "Unless your righteousness surpasses that of the scribes and Pharisees, you shall not enter the kingdom of heaven" (Matthew 5:20). Today, we might say, "You must first get someone lost before they can get saved."

The sermon relates to Bible prophecy in reference to the church age and the millennium. The sermon was not given directly to church-age believers since, in context, Christ is addressing entrance of the Jews into the kingdom. However, we can learn much about God's changeless character from the discourse. The kingdom will be brought to earth at the second coming of Christ. Many of the specific statements in this sermon will be fulfilled during the millennium.

Seven Churches of Revelation

Revelation 2–3 provides an inspection and report by Jesus Christ on seven churches that provide an overview of the course of this age. The perspective of these chapters is in reference to the program of the church, not the kingdom. Its overview proceeds from pentecost to the rapture as indicated by the often-repeated phrase, "He who has an ear, let him hear what the Spirit says to the churches" (Revelation 2:7,11,17,29; 3:6,13,22). These seven historical churches of the first century provide a pattern of the churches that will exist throughout church history.

Revelation 1:19 indicates a threefold division of the book of Revelation: "Write therefore the things which you have seen, and the things which are, and the things which shall take place after these things."

- *Revelation 1* corresponds with "the things which you have seen" and depicts the resurrected Christ.
- *Revelation 2–3* corresponds with "the things which are" and covers the church age.
- *Revelation 4–22* corresponds with "the things which shall take place after these things" and covers the tribulation, second coming, millennium, and eternal state.

It is clear from the above division of Revelation that the seven churches of Revelation 2–3 relate to the current church age. What lessons do these seven epistles to the churches teach us? G.H. Pember, a prophecy scholar of a previous generation, says,

Hence it seems clear, that the Churches selected must have been chosen because of their representative character. And, taking also into consideration the order in which they are placed, we may, probably, see in these Seven Epistles—apart from their literal application—a twofold purpose, affecting all the Churches of God's people upon earth.

For, firstly, if we regard them as a whole, we may, probably, detect in them specimens of every kind of circumstance, temptation, or trial, which God's foreknowledge saw in the future of Christian believers. Hence He is enabled, by means of them, to give advice, comfort, exhortation, or warning, to any of His Own disciples, and at any time during the course of the Church period.

And, secondly, if considered in the order in which they were given, they will be found to foreshadow the successive predominant phases through which the Nominal Church was to pass, from the time of the vision until the close of the Age. (*Great Prophecies,* pp. 494-95).

Bible students like Pember believe that the seven churches "present a prophetic picture of the seven historical periods in which the visible church will develop." This has been called "the historical-prophetical method of interpretation" (Fruchtenbaum, *Footsteps,* p. 38). Such an approach suggests that the church age will pass through these seven stages, providing a general prophetic outline beginning with Ephesus and concluding with Laodicea. The prophetic message is conveyed through the subject matter contained in each address, combined with the meaning of the names of the churches. These names characterize the particular period of church history in which they appear to find their fulfillment. Pember explains the names as follows:

Ephesus = relaxation. The waning of love at the close of Apostolic times.

Smyrna = bitterness; also myrrh, an unguent especially used for embalming the dead. The epoch of the Ten Great Persecutions.

Pergamum = a tower. Earthly greatness of the Nominal Church, from the accession of Constantine.

Thyatira = she that is unwearied in sacrifices. The Catholic Churches, with their perpetually repeated Sacrifice of the Mass.

Sardis = renovation. The results of the Reformation.

Philadelphia = brotherly love. The gathering in of those who believe the love of Christ to be a stronger bond of union than any ties of sect. This gathering evidently involves preparation for the Lord's return.

Laodicea = the custom, or judgment, of the people. The period in which the people constitute themselves judges of what is right, and so altogether set aside the Word of God. They are, consequently, rejected of the Lord Jesus.

(*Great Prophecies*, p. 497)

A typical outline of the prophetic aspects of the seven churches is provided by Dr. Arnold Fruchtenbaum:

1. Ephesus [A.D. 30–100] Apostolic Church
2. Smyrna [100–313] Roman Persecution
3. Pergamum [313–600] Age of Constantine
4. Thyatira [600–1517] Dark Ages
5. Sardis [1517–1648] Reformation
6. Philadelphia [1648–1900] Missionary Movement
7. Laodicea [1900–Present] Apostasy

(*Footsteps*, p. 36)

If such an approach is valid, it clearly indicates that history is in the final Laodicean era of the church age. Pember attempts to justify this viewpoint with the following explanation:

Again, if we turn to the Seventh Epistle, that to the Church of the Laodiceans, we perceive that it describes features which, according to other Scriptures, will characterize the closing days of this Age. For those who are addressed persist, indeed, in retaining a certain form of godliness, but neither regard its significance nor feel its power. They are self-satisfied and complacent on the very eve of judgment. And the Lord, Who is in the act of rejecting them, has withdrawn from their midst, and is only lingering for a moment at the door, to make a last offer to individual believers, and to utter a final warning (*Great Prophecies,* p. 496).

"But, if this be so, the question naturally arises," notes Pember, "Why did the Lord choose so peculiar a form for His revelation?" He provides the following answer:

Because He did not wish the prophetic import of the Epistles to be distinctly understood, until the Last Days had come. For, while these two chapters have been at all times most useful for reproof, correction, instruction, and exhortation, their predictions were scarcely likely to be discovered, or even suspected, until they were all but fulfilled. And so, they would never, by suggesting events that must first happen, cause believers to say, "My Lord delayeth His coming." And, on the other hand, when, at the time of the End, the Spirit should unveil their meaning, He would, by so doing, bring a deep conviction of the nearness of the Advent to every thoughtful and reverent mind.

And there is also another cause of obscuration in this form of prophecy. For, from the very nature of the case, such predictions cannot be direct and literal, as the prophecies of single events in the fourth and following chapters are, but can only dimly foreshadow things to come, though, if the clue be once obtained, with an outline sufficiently distinct.

Lastly, we must notice that in this prophecy, as in that of the Seven Parables, a phase that has once commenced may be continued, though often with contracted area, far beyond the time of its predominance, even, indeed, until the Lord's return. There is a plain intimation that this will be so in the case of Pergamum—for the Lord has not yet fought against the Balaamites with the sword of His mouth; in that of Thyatira—for the remnant are bidden to hold that fast which they have, until He come[s]; in that of Sardis—for she is told, that, unless she watches, He will come upon her as a thief; and in that of Philadelphia—for He promises her that He is coming quickly, and charges her to hold fast that which she has, that no one take her crown. Indeed, the Nominal Churches will, probably, in their last days, as in their first, embrace communities which, taken together, will exhibit all the characteristics mentioned in the two chapters; so that each of the Epistles will retain its directly practical value until the End. But, at that time, the prevailing phase will be the Laodicean (*Great Prophecies,* pp. 497–99).

This understanding of Revelation 2–3 indicates that the church has passed through her various stages and is now poised for the rapture to occur at any moment. However, only the general conclusion that we are in the final era is valid, since the Laodicean period could continue for hundreds of years, as did the Thyatiran age.

Shechinah Glory

The Shechinah glory is the visible manifestation of the presence of God, often showing up in the form of a cloud, light, fire, or combinations of these. The Jewish rabbis coined this extrabiblical expression. *Shechinah* is a form of a Hebrew word that literally means "he caused to dwell," signifying that when God's glory appeared in this way it was a divine visitation of the presence or dwelling of God. In order to see the significance of the Shechinah glory for future Bible prophecy, a survey of past appearances is necessary.

The following events are believed to be manifestations of the Shechinah glory in history:

- The Garden of Eden—the Lord's presence in the garden and the flaming sword (Genesis 3:8,23,24).
- The Abrahamic covenant—the flaming torch that passed between the sacrificial pieces (Genesis 15:12-18).
- The burning bush—the burning that did not consume the bush (Exodus 3:1-5).
- The exodus—the pillar of cloud by day and the pillar of fire by night (Exodus 13:21,22; 14:19,20,24; 16:6-12).
- Mount Sinai—the ten commandments written by the finger of God; thunder, lightning, and a thick cloud (Exodus 19:16-20; 24:15-18; Deuteronomy 5:22-27).
- The special meeting with Moses—the afterglow on Moses' face as a result of his meeting with the Lord (Exodus 33:17-23; 34:5-9,29-35).
- The tabernacle and the ark of the covenant—the glory-cloud presence often associated with these items (Exodus 29:42-46; 40:34-38).
- The book of Leviticus—the authentication of the law and residence in the holy of holies (Leviticus 9).
- The book of Numbers—the Shechinah glory rendered judgment for sin and disobedience (Numbers 13:30–14:45; 16:1-50; 20:5-13).
- The period of Joshua and Judges—the continued dwelling of the Shechinah glory in the tabernacle (1 Samuel 4:21,22).
- The Solomonic temple—the transfer of the Shechinah glory from the tabernacle to the temple (2 Chronicles 5:2–7:3).
- The departure in Ezekiel—Ezekiel watches the Shechinah glory depart the temple in preparation for judgment upon the nation (Ezekiel 1:28; 3:12,23; 8:3,4; 9:3; 10:4,18,19; 11:22,23).

- The second temple—the Shechinah glory was not present, but a promise was given that it will be greater in the future than in the past (Haggai 2:3,9).
- The appearance to the shepherds—the glory of the Lord shone around them (Luke 2:8,9).
- The star of Bethlehem—the star or glory-cloud that guided the magi to Jesus (Matthew 2:1-12).
- Jesus: The glory of the Lord—the incarnation was a manifestation of the Shechinah glory (John 1:1-14).
- The transfiguration—the Shechinah glory appears to the three disciples (Matthew 17:1-8; Mark 9:2-8; Luke 9:28-36; Hebrews 1:1-3; 2 Peter 1:16-18).
- The book of Acts—the cloven tongues of fire on pentecost and the blinding light shown upon Paul at his conversion (Acts 2:1-3; 9:3-8; 22:6-11; 26:13-18).
- The revelation—Jesus Christ is dressed in the Shechinah glory (Revelation 1:12-16).

The following is an overview of future events relating to the Shechinah glory.

- The tribulation—the Shechinah glory is connected with the bowl judgments (Revelation 15:8).
- The second coming of Christ—the Shechinah glory is the sign of the Son of Man and the cloud upon which He returns (Matthew 16:27; 24:30; Mark 13:26; Luke 21:27).
- The millennium—the Shechinah glory will be present in its greatest manifestation in history because of Christ's physical presence on earth (Ezekiel 43:1-7; 44:1,2; Isaiah 4:5,6; 11:10; 35:1,2; 40:5; 58:8,9; 60:1-3; Zechariah 2:4,5; 11:10).

S

- The eternal state—the Shechinah glory will provide light for the new creation where sin will be totally removed. God the Father, God the Son, and God the Holy Spirit will dwell in fullness with man (Revelation 21:1-3,10, 11,23,24).

(adapted from Fruchtenbaum, *Footsteps*, pp. 409-32)

See also "Clouds."

Sheol

In the Old Testament the Hebrew word *sheol* is used to describe hell. It occurs 65 times and is also translated into terms that include "hell," "pit," and "grave." *Sheol* can have different meanings in different contexts. It may refer to the grave (Job 17:13; Psalm 16:10; Isaiah 38:10). It also means the place to which the departed go (Genesis 37:35; 42:38; Numbers 16:33; Job 14:13; Psalm 55:15). Believers will be rescued from sheol (Psalm 16:9-11; 17:15; 49:15), but the wicked will not (Job 21:13; 24:19; Psalm 9:17; 31:17; 49:14; 55:15).

The major focus of the Old Testament is on the place where the bodies of people go, not where their souls exist. The destiny of the souls of individuals in the intermediate state is not expanded upon greatly in the Old Testament. The full doctrine of eternal destiny must be rounded out with the revelation of the New Testament. Sheol, though, is definitely a place of punishment (Job 24:19) and horror (Psalm 30:9).

See also "Hades."

Signs of the End of the Age

The rapture is the next prophesied event on God's prophetic calendar, but it is a signless event—there are not and never will be indicators that the rapture is near. This is true because the rapture is imminent; it could happen at any moment. Imminent events can't have signs since they couldn't happen until after the signs were present—eliminating the immediacy. Since the rapture is an event that could occur at any moment, it cannot be related to any signs at all. (See 1 Corinthians 1:7; 16:22; Philippians 3:20; 4:5; 1 Thessalonians 1:10; Titus 2:13; Hebrews 9:28; James 5:7-9; 1 Peter 1:13; Jude 21; Revelation 3:11; 22:7,12,17,20.) However, this does not mean that there are no general signs of the times that indicate the end of the age is drawing near. There are signs that relate to other aspects of God's plan that lead us to believe that the end of the age is upon us.

There are many signs that herald God's end-time program for Israel. However, we must be careful in how we see them relating to us. Since believers today live during the church age, prophetic signs relating to Israel are not being fulfilled in our day. Some prophecy teachers like to talk about how God is fulfilling dozens of prophecies in our day. This is not the case because the prophecies they cite refer to events that will take place during the tribulation. The world was prepared for Christ's first coming, so it will be prepared for events leading to His second coming. What God is doing in our day is preparing, or "stage-setting," the world for the time known as the tribulation.

Dr. John Walvoord explains:

But if there are no signs for the Rapture itself, what are the legitimate grounds for believing that the Rapture could be especially near of this generation?

The answer is not found in any prophetic events predicted before the Rapture but in understanding the events that will follow the Rapture. Just as history was prepared for Christ's first coming, in a similar way history is preparing for the events leading up to His Second Coming. . . . If this is the case, it leads to the inevitable conclusion that the Rapture may be excitingly near (*Armageddon,* p. 217).

PREPARATION FOR THE FULFILLMENT OF PROPHECY

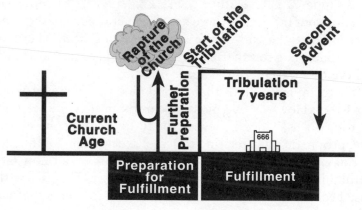

The Bible provides detailed prophecy about the seven-year tribulation. In fact, Revelation 4–19 gives a sequential outline of the major players and events. Using Revelation as a framework, we can harmonize the hundreds of other biblical passages that speak of the seven-year tribulation into a clear model of the next time period for planet Earth. With such a template to guide us, we can see that God is setting the stage for the great drama of the tribulation. One major indicator that we are likely near the beginning of the tribulation is the clear fact that national Israel has been reconstituted after almost 2,000 years. This future time casts shadows of expectation in our own day so that current events provide discernible signs of the times.

TIMING OF PROPHETIC FULFILLMENT

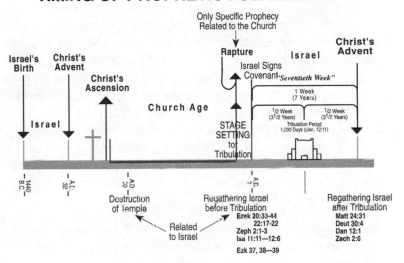

Six Hundred Sixty-Six (666)

In biblical symbolism and numerology, the number 666 is certainly one of the most significant items recorded. We read of this unique number in Revelation 13:16-18:

> And he [the Antichrist] causes all, the small and the great, and the rich and the poor, and the free men and the slaves, to be given a mark on their right hand, or on their forehead, and he provides that no one should be able to buy or to sell, except the one who has the mark, either the name of the beast or the

number of his name. Here is wisdom. Let him who has understanding calculate the number of the beast, for the number is that of a man; and his number is six hundred and sixty-six.

Probably no other number in history or in biblical studies has captivated the minds of both Christians and non-Christians as 666. Even those who know nothing of the future plan of God as revealed in the Bible know there is significance to this number. Too often, sincere students of prophecy have tied the number to contemporary technology and its potential in an effort to demonstrate the relevance of their interpretation. Yet to do so is to put the cart before the horse, for prophecy and the Bible do not gain authority or legitimacy because of our advances. The Bible is authoritative because it is the Word of God. We must allow the Bible to interpret and define culture and technology. Dr. John Walvoord writes of this enigmatic number:

> The Bible itself does not interpret the "666." Because in some languages the alphabet that is used has numerical value, some felt that this pointed to the beast as a character out of the past whose name in its numerical value would reveal the number "666." Accordingly, schemes abounded where many different names were suggested. . . . Though there may be more light cast on it at the time this prophecy is fulfilled, the passage itself declares that this number is "man's number." In the Book of Revelation the number "7" is one of the most significant numbers indicating perfection. Accordingly, there are seven seals, seven trumpets, seven bowls of the wrath of God, seven thunders, etc. This beast claims to be God, and if that were the case, he should be 777. This passage, in effect, says, No, you are only 666. You are short of deity even though you were originally created in the image and likeness of God. *Most of the speculation on the meaning of this number is*

S

without profit or theological significance (Prophecy Knowledge Handbook, p. 587, emphasis added).

In this same regard, Dr. Robert L. Thomas wisely notes:

> The identity of the person represented by the number 666 should not be a subject of speculation until that person arrives on the earthly scene. . . . It is true that 666 has a secondary implication regarding human limitation, but its primary meaning will be to help Christians of the future recognize the false Christ when he becomes a public figure (*Revelation 8–22*, pp. 183–84).

Dr. Arnold Fruchtenbaum has noted that interpretation of the mark will come as a result of understanding the following five clues:

- The name of the beast
- The number of his name
- The number of the beast
- The number of a man
- The number is 666

(*Footsteps*, p. 173)

Dr. Fruchtenbaum works through the clues as follows:

Following through this logical progression, the number of the beast is also the number of a man because the Antichrist will be a man who will be the last ruler of the final form of the fourth Gentile empire. Furthermore, this number is the number of his very own name, and the numerical value of his name is 666. The point is essentially this: whatever the name of the Antichrist will be in Hebrew, the numerical value of that name will be 666. Each letter in the Hebrew alphabet has a numerical value. . . . In this passage whatever the personal name of the Antichrist will be, if his name is spelled out in

Hebrew characters, the numerical value of his name will be 666. So this is the number that will be put on the worshippers of the Antichrist. Since a number of different calculations can equal 666, it is impossible to figure the name out in advance. But when he does appear, whatever his personal name will be, it will equal 666. Those who are wise (verse 18) at that time will be able to point him out in advance (*Footsteps,* p. 173).

See the chart below for the numerical values in the Hebrew alphabet.

Numerical Value of the Hebrew Alphabet

א – 1	ט – 9	ע – 70
ב – 2	י – 10	פ – 80
ג – 3	כ – 20	צ – 90
ד – 4	ל – 30	ק – 100
ה – 5	מ – 40	ר – 200
ו – 6	נ – 50	שׁ – 300
ז – 7	ס – 60	ת – 400
ח – 8		

Statue of Daniel 2

In the sixth century B.C., Nebuchadnezzar, king of the most powerful empire in the world, had a dream. It just so happened that Daniel, a Hebrew, was available to reveal and interpret the dream.

Daniel 2:31-35 revealed the vision of a large statue of a man whose body parts were made of different metals. The head was of pure gold, the chest area and arms were of silver, the hips and thighs were made of bronze, the legs were made of iron, and the feet were composed of iron and baked clay. Next, Daniel saw a large stone that was cut out of a mountain without human hands. It struck the feet of the figure, toppling and destroying the whole statue. Finally, the stone that destroyed the statue became a huge mountain that filled the whole earth.

Daniel explains the meaning of the dream in verses 36-45. He points out that history will be dominated by the rise to world power of a series of Gentile nations. These Gentile nations will rule the world until they are destroyed by a fifth and final kingdom—God's kingdom involving national Israel. The period of Gentile domination and the four kingdoms, which started with the rise of Babylon in 586 B.C., is called "the times of the Gentiles." This time period will last until God smashes the final forms of the kingdoms of man in the last days.

Nebuchadnezzar and Babylon are the first Gentile kingdom, represented by the head of gold. The next kingdom that will arise is Medo-Persia, represented by the silver upper body. The third kingdom made of bronze will be Greece, and the legs of iron represent Rome. The feet of iron and baked clay represent a yet future revived Roman empire coming from the fourth kingdom (from which the Antichrist arises during the tribulation). The stone cut out of the mountain without hands refers to Christ who, at His second coming, will smash the Antichrist and his kingdom and will set up His worldwide rule known as the millennial kingdom.

The following is a summary of the four kingdoms represented in the statue:

- *Babylon* (612–539 B.C.)—represented by the head of gold (Daniel 2:32)
- *Medo-Persia* (539–331 B.C.)—represented by the silver upper body (Daniel 2:32)
- *Greece* (331–63 B.C.)—represented by the belly and thighs made of bronze (Daniel 2:32)
- *Rome* (63 B.C.–A.D. 476; revived Roman empire during the tribulation)—represented by legs of iron and feet mixed with iron and brittle clay (Daniel 2:33).

The following is a depiction of the statue found in Nebuchadnezzar's dream and the various kingdoms it represents.

NEBUCHADNEZZAR'S STATUE

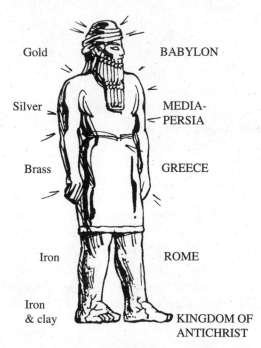

Stone Cut Without Hands

In the vision, the large stone cut out of a mountain without human hands struck the feet of a statue and totally destroyed the image (Daniel 2). Then this stone became a huge mountain and filled the whole earth. The "stone cut without hands" is a picture of Christ's millennial kingdom. It is cut without hands signifying it is a kingdom of divine origin, in contrast to the four phases of the kingdom of man that the stone destroyed. Set within the prophetic framework, the stone means that Christ will judge the Antichrist's kingdom during the tribulation. At this time He will crush it and wipe it out forever, preparing the way for His millennial reign and, eventually, His eternal kingdom in the new heavens and new earth.

T

Tartaros

In 2 Peter 2:4 the word *hell* is translated from the word *Tartaros*. It refers to a place where certain, but not all, fallen angels (demons) are confined. The word was used in classical mythology for a subterranean abyss in which rebellious gods were punished. It came over into Hellenistic Judaism, and it was used also in the apocryphal book of Enoch (2:20) in reference to fallen angels.

Temple

The English word *temple* is derived from the Latin term *templum,* which is a translation of the Hebrew noun *hekal,* meaning "big house." In the Bible, *temple* usually refers to the Jerusalem temple. Scripture also speaks of a heavenly temple. Isaiah was caught up to heaven and describes a scene that could well be the heavenly temple: "I saw the Lord sitting on a throne. . . . Seraphim stood above Him. . . . The temple was filled with smoke" (Isaiah 6). John, having been caught up into heaven, specifically speaks of a "heavenly temple" from which God oversees the judgments of the tribulation and sends forth His angels: "They are before the throne of God; and they serve Him day and night in His temple" (Revelation 7:15; see also 11:19; 14:15,17; 15:5,6, 8; 16:1,17). The heavenly temple, in some ways, serves as the model for the various earthly dwellings of God (that is, the tabernacle, temple, and spiritual temple—the church).

The Bible speaks of four temples in Jerusalem. The first two temples, Solomon's and Herod's, have already been built and destroyed. The final two temples, the tribulation temple and the millennial temple, are yet to be built and are spoken of in great detail in biblical prophecy. The last of these, the millennial temple, will be erected by the Lord Jesus when He returns to establish His messianic kingdom. In the eternal state there is no temple because the new heavens and new earth are not polluted with sin; therefore, the Holy God is able to dwell openly with man.

The Tribulation Temple The fact that there will be a third Jewish temple in Jerusalem, at least by the midpoint of the seven-year tribulation period, is supported by at least four scriptural references:

- *Daniel 9:27:* This passage predicts a future time-period of seven years, during which the Antichrist defiles Israel's temple at the three-and-a-half-year point. (In order for this to happen, there must be a temple in Jerusalem.)
- *Matthew 24:15,16:* In this passage, Jesus speaks of "the abomination of desolation . . . standing in the holy place." "The holy place" is a reference to the most sacred room within Israel's temple. What temple? The third one, since it is a future event. (This is the same event referred to in Daniel 9:27.)
- *2 Thessalonians 2:3,4:* In this passage we see, for the third time, a description of "the abomination of desolation." This time it is referred to as the event in which Antichrist "takes his seat in the temple of God." Once again, which one? The clear answer is the future third temple.
- *Revelation 11:1,2:* Since the section of Revelation in which this passage appears takes place during the tribulation period, this must be a reference to Israel's third temple in Jerusalem.

This tribulation temple is also called Antichrist's temple because he will defile it by setting up his image in the Holy of

Holies. This blasphemous act is "the abomination of desolation" (Daniel 9:27; 11:31; 12:11; Matthew 24:15; Mark 13:14; 2 Thessalonians 2:4; Revelation 13:15).

The tribulation temple will play a central role in Israel's national restoration during the seven years of tribulation, which prepares the nation for acceptance of Jesus as Messiah just prior to the second advent. The biblical role for the third temple relates to an apostate restoration of Israel's worship system during the tribulation. Such a restoration provides the platform for Antichrist to challenge and insult God, who responds in judgment from His heavenly temple.

The Millennial Temple In Ezekiel 40–48, the Bible teaches that there will be a fourth temple. This final temple will be the center from which worship of Jesus Christ during the millennium will be focused. Destined to be perhaps the most beautiful and magnificent building in human history, the fourth, or millennial, temple is discussed in detail in Ezekiel 40:5–43:27. The Old Testament also refers to sacrifices that will take place in this temple in the following passages: Isaiah 56:5-7; 60:7; 66:20; Jeremiah 33:15; Zechariah 14:16-21.

The millennial temple will be the focus of the entire world during Christ's 1,000-year reign from Jerusalem. Israel and the temple will serve as the center for the priestly rituals and offerings that will provide guidance in the worship of Jesus the Messiah. Since this will be a time in which Israel will be exalted and Christ will rule the world through a theocracy from Jerusalem, it makes sense that worship of Messiah will revolve around a temple. As Israel fulfills her national calling, the glory of the Lord will return to the temple (Ezekiel 43:1-5).

Israel's Four Temples

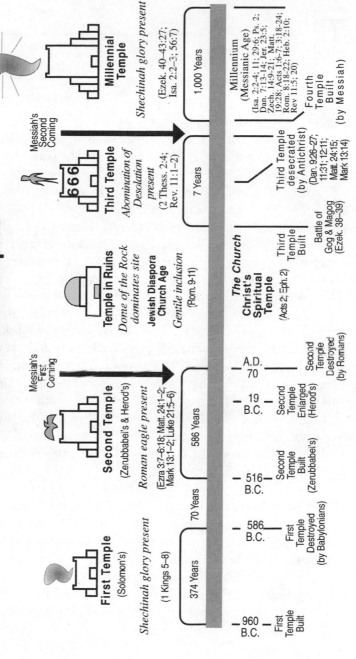

First Temple (Solomon's)

Shechinah glory present

(1 Kings 5–8)

Second Temple (Zerubbabel's & Herod's)

Roman eagle present

(Ezra 3:7–6:18; Matt. 24:1–2; Mark 13:1–2; Luke 21:5–6)

Messiah's First Coming

Temple in Ruins

Dome of the Rock dominates site

Jewish Diaspora Church Age

Gentile inclusion

(Rom. 9–11)

Third Temple

Abomination of Desolation present

(2 Thess. 2:4; Rev. 11:1–2)

Messiah's Second Coming

Millennial Temple

Shechinah glory present

(Ezek. 40–43:27; Isa. 2:2–3; 56:7)

374 Years | 70 Years | 586 Years | 7 Years | 1,000 Years

960 B.C. — First Temple Built

586 B.C. — First Temple Destroyed (by Babylonians)

516 B.C. — Second Temple Built (Zerubbabel's)

19 B.C. — Second Temple Enlarged (Herod's)

A.D. 70 — Second Temple Destroyed (by Romans)

The Church **Christ's Spiritual Temple**

(Acts 2; Eph. 2)

Third Temple Built

Battle of Gog & Magog (Ezek. 38–39)

Third Temple desecrated (by Antichrist)

(Dan. 9:26–27; 11:31; 12:11; Matt. 24:15; Mark 13:14)

Millennium (Messianic Age)

(Isa. 2:2–4; 11; 29:6; Ps. 2; Dan. 7:13–14; Jer. 23:5; Zech. 14:9–21; Matt. 19:28; Acts 1:6–7; 3:18–24; Rom. 8:18–22; Heb. 2:10; Rev 11:5; 20)

Fourth Temple Built (by Messiah)

Ten-Horned Beast

A ten-horned beast is revealed in Daniel 7:19,20. Daniel explains, "As for the ten horns, out of this kingdom ten kings will arise" (verse 24). These ten kings shall appear during the final phase of the fourth beast's empire, which is the tribulation period yet to come. This many-headed beast is the same as the ten toes of Nebuchadnezzar's image mentioned in Daniel 2:42. (See also "Statue of Daniel 2.")

In concert with Daniel, John tells us, "And the ten horns which you saw are ten kings, who have not yet received a kingdom, but they receive authority as kings with the beast for one hour" (Revelation 17:12). Earlier, John "saw a beast coming up out of the sea, having ten horns and seven heads, and on his horns were ten diadems, and on his heads were blasphemous names" (13:1). This is descriptive of Antichrist and his kingdom during the tribulation. The ten horns represent ten powers or kingdoms. The ten diadems on the heads represent the ten kings over the kingdoms. And the blasphemous names tell us that each ruler is in league with Antichrist in his opposition to God. The ten-horned beast is the biblical description of the ten nations who, at some point in the tribulation, will make up the power base of the Antichrist's kingdom. Dr. John Walvoord explains:

> The prediction that there will be a ten-kingdom stage of the revival of the Roman Empire is one of the important descriptive prophecies of the end time. This prophecy anticipates that there will be ten countries originally related to the Roman Empire that will constitute the Roman Empire in its revived form. . . . The prediction requires a political union and then a dictator over the ten countries (*Major Bible Prophesies,* pp. 314–15).

Ten-Nation Confederacy
The ten-nation confederacy is the ten toes of Daniel's image in Daniel 2:42. It pictures the final form of the fourth kingdom during the tribulation.

See also "Revived Roman Empire," "Statue of Daniel," and "Ten-Horned Beast."

Time of Jacob's Trouble
The phrase "the time of Jacob's trouble" (KJV) or "the time of Jacob's distress" (NASB) comes from the prophecy found in Jeremiah 30:7. It refers to the Antichrist's persecution of the Jews during the tribulation. In this passage, the prophet Jeremiah speaks of a yet-future time when great distress or tribulation will come upon all Israel, symbolically referred to as "Jacob." Biblical expositor and prophecy scholar Dr. Charles H. Dyer writes of this passage and its meaning:

> To what "time of trouble" was Jeremiah referring? Some have felt that he was pointing to the coming fall of Judah to Babylon or to the later fall of Babylon to Medo-Persia. However, in both of these periods the Northern Kingdom of Israel was not affected. It had already gone into captivity (in 722 B.C.). A better solution is to see Jeremiah referring to the still-future Tribulation period when the remnant of Israel and Judah will experience a time of unparalleled persecution (Daniel 9:27; 12:1; Matthew 24:15-22). The period will end when Christ appears to rescue His elect (Romans 11:26) and establish His kingdom (Matthew 24:30-31; 25:31-46; Revelation 19:11-21; 20:4-6) ("Jeremiah," *Bible Knowledge Commentary*, p. 1168).

"The time of Jacob's distress" emphasizes the aspect of the future tribulation that focuses upon the difficulty that Jews, the descendants of Jacob, will experience. This expression tells us that one of the major themes of the tribulation will centers on Israel and that the nation will pass through this time so that, as Jeremiah concludes, Israel "will be saved from it" (30:7).

Times and Seasons

Times means "duration of times, dates" and "seasons" (or "epochs" [NASB]) refers to "periods of critical importance." As a word pair, they relate to knowing when significant prophetic events will happen. Daniel tells us "He changeth the times and the seasons" (Daniel 2:21 KJV). Christ told His disciples at His ascension, when asked if the kingdom of God would be restored to Israel at this time, "It is not for you to know the times or the seasons, which the Father hath put in his own power" (Acts 1:7 KJV). Paul tells the Thessalonians, "But of the times and the seasons, brethren, ye have no need that I write unto you" (1 Thessalonians 5:1 KJV).

Times of Refreshing

Peter bids his fellow Israelites to accept Jesus as the Messiah "in order that times of refreshing may come from the presence of the Lord" (Acts 3:19). This phrase refers to the millennium. Indeed, after the trials of the tribulation, the millennium will certainly be a refreshing time for the nation of Israel.

Times of the Gentiles

The phrase "times of the Gentiles" is found in Luke 21:24 and refers to the period of Gentile domination of Jerusalem. This era began in circa 586 B.C., when Nebuchadnezzar exerted Babylonian, and thus, Gentile domination over

Jerusalem. This domination lasted through the destruction of Jerusalem in A.D. 70, and will continue through the tribulation. The "times of the Gentiles" did not end when the modern state of Israel captured Jerusalem in 1967, as some teach, because the city will be under Gentile rule during parts of the tribulation. During the second half of the tribulation (the great tribulation), the Jews will again be persecuted and driven out of Jerusalem. This time period will be the ultimate "times of the Gentiles" under the control and persecution of the Antichrist. It will end at the second coming of Jesus Christ and the setting up of His glorious millennial reign. From that time on, Jerusalem will never again be subjected to Gentile domination.

Times, Times, and Half a Time

This phrase refers to the last three-and-a-half years of the tribulation. According to Daniel 7:25; 12:7; and Revelation 12:14, this era, known also as the great tribulation, comes after the Antichrist breaks a covenant with Israel and begins a time of intense persecution. From Daniel 4:25, it is understood that *times* equals years. Therefore, in this phrase time equals one year, times equals two years, and half a time equals half a year. The three-and-a-half-year calculation receives further confirmation from other time designations: 42 months (Revelation 11:2; 13:5), 1,260 days (Revelation 11:3; 12:6)—all signifying three-and-a-half years.

Tribulation

The tribulation in Bible prophecy is the seven-year period of time between the rapture of the church and the second coming of Jesus Christ. The most extensive biblical comments on the tribulation are found in the writings of John, specifically in Revelation 6–19. In these chapters, John provides a detailed exposition of the tribulation days. Daniel's "70 weeks" (Daniel 9:24-27) are the framework within which the tribulation or the seventieth week occurs. The seven-year period of Daniel's seventieth week is a time span to which a host of descriptives are associated. Some of those descriptive terms include: tribulation, great tribulation, day of the Lord, day of wrath, day of distress, day of trouble, time of Jacob's distress, day of darkness and gloom, and wrath of the Lamb.

God's basic purpose for the tribulation is that it be a time of judgment, although, at the same time, He will hold forth the gospel of grace. This will precede Christ's glorious 1,000-year reign from David's throne in Jerusalem. God's purpose for the tribulation can be divided into three aspects:

- To make an end of wickedness and wicked ones (Isaiah 13:9; 24:19,20)—The first purpose for the tribulation is seen to be a punishment in history upon the whole world for its sins against God, in a way similar to that of the global flood in Noah's days (Matthew 24:37-39).
- To bring about a worldwide revival—This purpose is given and fulfilled in Revelation 7:1-17. During the first half of the tribulation, God will evangelize the world by the means of the 144,000 Jews and thus fulfill the prophecy found in Matthew 24:14.
- To break the power of the holy people—Israel—Finally, the tribulation will be a time in which God, through evil agencies, prepares Israel for her conversion and acknowledgment that Jesus is their Messiah, resulting in the second coming of Christ.

(Fruchtenbaum, *Footsteps*, pp. 122–26)

One of the most important passages for the study of the future is Daniel 9:24-27. In these four verses Daniel provides a clear and concise framework for prophetic study:

Seventy weeks have been decreed . . . to finish the transgression, to make an end of sin, to make atonement for iniquity, to bring in everlasting righteousness, to seal up vision and prophecy, and to anoint the most holy place. So you are to know and discern that from the issuing of a decree to restore and rebuild Jerusalem until Messiah the Prince there will be seven weeks and sixty-two weeks. . . .

Then after the sixty-two weeks the Messiah will be cut off and have nothing, and the people of the prince who is to come will destroy the city and the sanctuary. And its end will come with a flood; even to the end there will be war; desolations are determined. And he will make a firm covenant with the many for one week, but in the middle of the week he will put a stop to sacrifice and grain offering; and on the wing of abominations will come one who makes desolate, even until a complete destruction, one that is decreed, is poured out on the one who makes desolate.

A proper understanding of these verses gives students of the Bible scriptural signposts for biblical prophecy. From this passage we learn that the tribulation is a seven-year period divided by the "abomination of desolation" into two three-and-a-half-year periods. (The "week" that Daniel writes of is understood by most prophecy scholars to be a "week of years" or seven years.) These years follow the interval of the "seven weeks and sixty-two weeks" found in Daniel 9:25. In Daniel 9:2, Daniel was thinking about the years of Israel's captivity by the Babylonians. This captivity had been prophesied by Jeremiah as being a period of 70 years (Jeremiah 25:11,12; 29:10).

As Daniel studied the words of Jeremiah and prayed (Daniel 9:3-19), the angel Gabriel appeared to him revealing the prophetic timetable found in Daniel 9:24-27. The Hebrew term used for "weeks" in this passage literally means "sevens" or "units of seven" without specifying whether it means days, months, or years. However, in this passage only "years" fits the timetable since a period of 490 days or 490 months is historically too short a time span. The 70 weeks must be a period of 490 years (70 × 7). The seventieth week must also be a period of seven years. Dr. Walvoord writes:

> The only system of interpretation, however, that gives any literal meaning to this prophecy is to regard the time units as prophetic years of 360 days each according to the Jewish custom of having years of 360 days with an occasional extra month inserted to correct the calendar as needed. The seventy times seven is therefore 490 years with the beginning at the time of "the commandment to restore and rebuild Jerusalem" found in verse 25 and the culmination of 490 years later in verse 27. Before detailing the events between the sixty-ninth seven and the seventieth seven, and the final seven years, Daniel gives the overall picture in verse 24. Careful attention must be given to the precise character of this important foundational prophecy *(Daniel,* pp. 219–20).

Building upon an Old Testament foundation, the New Testament expands our picture of the tribulation. The first extended passage we find dealing with the tribulation in the New Testament are the words of Jesus in Matthew 24:4-28 (see also Mark 13; Luke 17:22-37; and Luke 21:5-36). In this discourse, Jesus describes the tribulation period. In verses 4-14, He speaks about the first half of the tribulation, and in verses 15-28, He describes the second half leading up to the second coming. According to Jesus, the tribulation will be intense and extensive and will include both human and natural disasters. Jesus then told the disciples that the second half of the tribulation would be no better than the first half. In fact, the trauma and suffering would escalate to such a point that it would end only after the battle of Armageddon and the second coming of Christ.

Paul's Thessalonian epistles also deal extensively with prophetic information and the tribulation. Twice Paul refers to the tribulation when speaking of a future time of wrath (1 Thessalonians 1:10; 5:9; see also Romans 5:9). In 2 Thessalonians 2:1,2, Paul tells his readers that they should not be deceived into thinking that the tribulation (the day of the Lord) had already started. He continues, in verses 3-13, to expound on some of the events of the tribulation era.

According to the prophetic timeline of Daniel 9:24-27 and 2 Thessalonians 2, the tribulation will follow the rapture of the church. This event, which is yet future, will terminate the present interval between the sixty-ninth and seventieth weeks of Daniel and allow the tribulation to begin.

The tribulation will not begin the day the church is raptured, as some people erroneously think. There will be a stage-setting interval between the rapture and the start of the tribulation. The tribulation actually begins with the signing of a covenant between the leader of the revived Roman empire, and based in Europe, the nation of Israel. This event will set into motion the countdown of events we know as the tribulation. (The following events of the tribulation are adapted from Fruchtenbaum, *Footsteps,* pp. 135–91.)

Events of the First Half of the Tribulation

1. *The Seal Judgments*—Revelation 6 outlines the seven seal judgments (the seventh contains the trumpet judgments) that kick off the tribulation. The first four seals are also known as the four horsemen of the apocalypse. These judgments are the beginnings of the wrath of God that is directed at the earth.

2. *The Rise of Antichrist and the Ten-Nation Confederacy*—Since the beginning of the tribulation will be marked by

the signing of a covenant between Israel and the Antichrist (Daniel 9:26,27), it makes sense that he will come on the scene in the first half of the tribulation. He will be the head of a ten-nation confederacy that will rule the world during the tribulation (see Daniel 2:42,44; 7:7,24; Revelation 12:3; 13:1; 17:12,16).

3. *The Ministry of Elijah*—The ministry of Elijah, which could be fulfilled through the ministry of the two witnesses (Revelation 11:3), will be one of restoration toward the nation of Israel (Malachi 4:5,6). Since it will be "before the coming of the great and terrible day of the LORD," it will occur in the first half of the tribulation.

4. *The Revival Through the 144,000 Jewish Evangelists*—Revelation 7 details the call and ministry of 144,000 Jewish evangelists, who preach the gospel during the first half of the tribulation.

5. *The Trumpet Judgments*—Revelation 8 and 9 speak of the trumpet judgments. As with the seal judgments, the seventh trumpet contains the final series of judgments known as the bowl judgments. These judgments focus on nature and include two of the three woe judgments.

6. *The Ministry of the Two Witnesses*—Just as the 144,000 Jews are engaged in world evangelism, the two witnesses are sealed by God to be a special witness to Jerusalem and Israel (Revelation 11:3-6).

7. *The False Church*—Also known as "Ecclesiastical Babylon." The false church will have great power and influence during the first half of the tribulation (Revelation 17:1-6). It will aid the Antichrist in his deception.

Events of the Middle of the tribulation

1. *The Little Scroll*—The apostle John is commanded by the interpreting angel to eat the scroll in Revelation 10:9.

T

The content of the scroll is prophecy relating to the middle and second half of the tribulation. Biblical prophecy is considered good (sweet) by many people, but the message of judgment is hard (bitter) to take.

2. *The Antichrist Is Killed*—Revelation 13:3 notes that the seventh head (a reference to Antichrist) is killed but miraculously revived.

3. *Satan Cast Down to Earth from Heaven*—Revelation 12:7-9 reveals that Satan himself is cast to the earth through angelic agency. This provides the basis for an intensification of events upon earth during the second half of the tribulation.

4. *The Resurrection of the Antichrist*—One of the first things Satan does on earth, after being cast out of heaven is to resurrect the Antichrist. Revelation 13:3,4 records the Antichrist's attempts to counterfeit the career of Jesus the Messiah.

5. *Three Kings Killed; Seven Submit*—After his death and resurrection, Antichrist consolidates his worldwide rule by killing three of the ten kings, which leads to the other seven kings submitting voluntarily. This event provides the political base from which Antichrist will project his power during the last half of the tribulation (Revelation 17:12,13).

6. *Destruction of the False Church*—As has often been the case historically, when a tyrant reaches his goal of total political control he destroys those who helped him reach that point. Antichrist now destroys the harlot, ecclesiastical Babylon (Revelation 17:16).

7. *The Death and Resurrection of the Two Witnesses*—God enables the temporary deception of Antichrist to proceed further with the death of the "two witnesses." During the first half of the tribulation the two witnesses were miraculously protected by God. God now allows the deception of Antichrist to deepen. The Antichrist murders the two witnesses in Jerusalem, and the whole world rejoices. However,

after three-and-one-half days the two witnesses will be resurrected and taken to heaven in the sight of all. Fear then grips those who have followed after the beast (Revelation 11:7-13).

8. *The Worship of the Antichrist*—Since the "earth dwellers" prefer the counterfeit over the genuine, they will be deceived into worshiping the Antichrist as God. In reality they will be worshiping Satan (Revelation 13:3,4,8).

9. *The False Prophet*—This person is a counterfeit of the ministry of the Holy Spirit. He is temporarily empowered to do false signs, wonders, and miracles which greatly aid the Antichrist's rise to power. False religion is the vehicle of deception for this second beast, the False Prophet (Revelation 13:11-15).

10. *666: The Mark of the Beast*—Another "ministry" of the False Prophet will be the administering of the counterfeit seal of the Holy Spirit—the famous mark of the beast—"666." Placement of this mark on the forehead or right hand will be required to conduct economic transactions during the second half of the tribulation. It should be noted that any person receiving this mark cannot be saved. This mark will not be distributed during the first half of the tribulation, only during the latter half. Since the meaning of 666 is a mystery, it is not wise to speculate as to its meaning until the time in which it is distributed. Its meaning will be clear to believers during the tribulation (Revelation 13:16-18).

11. *The Seven-Year Covenant Broken*—It is not at all surprising that the Antichrist will break his covenant with Israel. Such a move is in keeping with his character. This betrayal will involve his military invasion of Israel (Isaiah 28:18; Daniel 11:41).

12. *The Abomination of Desolation*—Antichrist will not only break his covenant with Israel, he will set himself up as God and expect to be worshiped in the rebuilt Jewish temple.

This defiling act of the third temple, at the midpoint of the tribulation, is called "the abomination of desolation." This will be a sign to the Jews to flee Jerusalem (Daniel 9:27; Matthew 24:15,16; 2 Thessalonians 2:4).

13. *The Persecution of the Jews*—The second half of the tribulation will be characterized by an extreme attempt to wipe the Jews off the face of the earth. Likely, Satan's thinking on this matter is that if the Jews are exterminated, then God's plan for history will have been thwarted. Satan might think this would somehow prevent the second coming. This persecution is pictured in Revelation 12:1-6. Within this imagery, the woman represents Israel and her male child represents Christ.

Events of the Second Half of the Tribulation

1. *The Bowl Judgments*—The bowl judgment series is the most severe judgment of the tribulation. The bowl judgments occur in the second half of the tribulation and devastate Antichrist's kingdom, preparing the way for the second coming of Christ. These judgments are the result of the prayers of the saints for God to take revenge on their behalf (Revelation 6:10; 15). The bowl judgments are described in Revelation 16.

2. *The Protection of the Jewish Remnant*—At the midpoint of the tribulation the Jews will flee when Antichrist commits the abomination of desolation. Apparently these Jews will be protected in the Jordanian village of Bozrah, known also as Petra. This is one way a remnant will be preserved (Micah 2:12; Matthew 24:16; Revelation 12:6,14).

3. *Armageddon: The Assembling of the Allies of Antichrist* (Revelation 16:12-16).

4. *Armageddon: The Destruction of Babylon* (Isaiah 13; Jeremiah 50–51; Revelation 18).

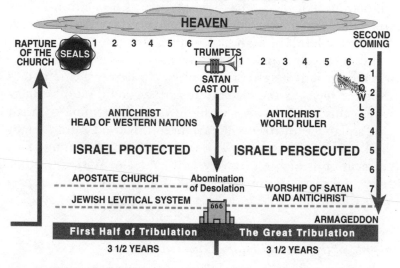

5. *Armageddon: The Fall of Jerusalem* (Micah 4:11–5:1; Zechariah 12:1-9; 14:1,2).

6. *Armageddon: The Armies of Antichrist at Bozrah* (Jeremiah 49:13,14).

7. *The Conversion of Israel*—Right before the second coming Israel will be converted to belief in the messiahship of Jesus and be saved from its sins. This will prepare it for its role in the millennial kingdom after the second advent (Zechariah 12:10; Romans 11:25-27).

Such detail in this overview of the tribulation events is not surprising since the seven years of the tribulation are covered as extensively by the Bible as any period in history. All of these events culminate in the second coming of Jesus Christ.

Tribulation Martyrs

Revelation 6:9-11 speaks of the opening of the fifth seal judgment and the martyrdom of tribulation saints. These persecuted saints are not part of the church, which is already in heaven at this time. Rather, these are individuals who receive Jesus Christ after the rapture and during the early part of the tribulation. According to Revelation 7:9, people from every nation will be converted during the tribulation. Yet it will also be a time of persecution and martyrdom for many who accept Jesus Christ. Revelation 6:9 speaks of them as "souls underneath the altar," since in the Old Testament the blood of sacrifices was poured under the altar (Exodus 29:12; Leviticus 4:7). In Revelation 6:10 John hears them cry out asking why God has not avenged their deaths and judged their persecutors. The reply is in 6:11, where they are told that it will be a short time longer so that the plan of God can be completed. This short time period is the remainder of the tribulation. Dr. John Walvoord writes:

> The revelation of the fifth seal makes clear that in the future time of tribulation it will be most difficult to declare one's faith in the Lord Jesus. It may very well be that the majority of those who trust Christ as Savior in that day will be put to death. This is confirmed in chapter 7, where another picture of the martyred dead of the tribulation is given, and in chapter 13, where death is inflicted on all who will not worship the beast. Martyrdom in those days will be as common as it is uncommon today. Thousands will be martyred, sealing their testimony with their own blood. Those who trust in Christ in that day will be forced to stand the acid test of being faithful even unto death (*The Revelation,* p. 134).

The martyred saints will be raised at the end of the tribulation and will enter into the blessing of the millennial kingdom

(Revelation 20:4-6). It is at this time that they will receive their resurrection bodies.

Tribulation Saints

This is an extrabiblical term to designate those individuals who become believers during the tribulation. Revelation 7:9 speaks of them:

> After these things I looked, and behold, a great multitude, which no one could count, from every nation and all tribes and peoples and tongues, standing before the throne and before the Lamb, clothed in white robes, and palm branches were in their hands.

Trumpet Judgments

The second of the three series of seven judgments that take place during the tribulation is known as trumpet judgments (Revelation 8–9; 11:15). A trumpet was used in the ancient world to signal a special announcement or the advent of a major event. These judgments certainly qualify as major events. The judgments are all administered by special angels, and the movement is from heaven to earth—clearly showing that it is God, not nature, that is the origin of these afflictions. Many of these judgments are similar to the ten plagues on Egypt found in Exodus 7–11. The seven trumpet judgments are as follows:

- *First Trumpet* (Revelation 8:7)—The first trumpet judgment is hail and fire mixed with blood that was thrown down upon the earth with the result that "a third of the earth was burned up, and a third of the trees were burned up, and all the green grass was burned up." Many have seen parallels with the Old Testament judgments of Sodom and Gomorrah (Genesis 18:16–19:28) and the sixth plague upon Egypt in the exodus (Exodus 9:22-26).

- *Second Trumpet* (Revelation 8:8,9)—The second trumpet judgment involves something "like a great mountain burning with fire" being thrown into the sea so that "a third of the sea became blood; and a third of the creatures, which were in the sea and had life, died; and a third of the ships were destroyed." This judgment has similarities with the first plague in Egypt (Exodus 7:16-21).

- *Third Trumpet* (Revelation 8:10,11)—The third trumpet judgment is "a great star" falling from heaven, "burning like a torch, and it fell on a third of the rivers and on the springs of waters." The star is named Wormwood (meaning "bitter") and could be an angelic entity since it has a proper name and stars are sometimes associated with angels (Revelation 1:10; Job 38:7). Many die from the bitter water.

- *Fourth Trumpet* (Revelation 8:12,13)—The fourth trumpet judgment smites the heavens so that a third of the sun, moon, and stars are diminished. This judgment parallels the ninth plague on Egypt (Exodus 10:21-23). In association with this judgment comes an angelic announcement to the earth concerning the three remaining trumpet judgments.

- *Fifth Trumpet* (Revelation 9:1-11)—The fifth trumpet judgment involves another star falling to earth from heaven, but this one, likely Satan himself, has the key to the bottomless pit, which he opens and looses a great swarm of demonic locusts. These special creatures are permitted to torture—but not kill—people for five months. This demonic locust invasion is also spoken of in Joel 2:1-11. It will be a terrible time to be an unbeliever.

- *Sixth Trumpet* (Revelation 9:13-21)—The sixth trumpet judgment releases four angels who are specially created for this moment in history. They are tasked with killing a third of the people on earth. These angels command an angelic host of 200 million demons who go forth as horsemen to inflict death. (These are not 200 million Chinese, as has been suggested by some—they are clearly of demonic origin.) They, like the creatures for the previous judgment, come from the bottomless pit and are clearly not human. By this time in history, at least half of the earth's population will have died in only a few years. Scripture reports that they "did not repent of the works of their hands, so as not to worship demons, and the idols . . ."

TRUMPET JUDGMENTS

HEAVEN

RAPTURE
OF THE
CHURCH

TRUMPET JUDGMENTS

SECOND
COMING

SEALS

hail, fire
1
upon earth

sun, moon, stars
4
upon heavens

7 bowls
7

burning mountain
2
upon sea

demonic locust
5
upon people

BOWLS

Wormwood
3
upon waters

horsemen
6
upon people

666

The Great Tribulation

3 1/2 YEARS

- *Seventh Trumpet* (Revelation 11:15-19)—The seventh trumpet judgment is the seven bowl judgments that follow.

See also "Bowl Judgments."

Twenty-Four Elders

The 24 elders are spoken of in Revelation 4:4 and 19:4. They are in heaven during the tribulation and represent humanity in their initiatives and responses. The identity of the elders is not specifically given, although there are two major views regarding their identity: 1) they represent the church, which has been raptured prior to this time and rewarded; and 2) they are angelic beings (though nowhere else in the Bible are angels said to be given crowns and rewards). The first view is the more sensible one.

Two Witnesses

According to Revelation 11:3-14, there will arise two unique witnesses proclaiming the gospel for a period of 1,260 days during the tribulation. Their supernatural ministry is related to Jerusalem and the nation of Israel, in which they perform a special witness to God's program of judgment.

Most prophecy teachers have identified these two witnesses as Moses and Elijah (or perhaps Enoch and Elijah). Both Moses and Elijah were involved in the transfiguration that anticipated the second coming of Jesus Christ (Matthew 17:3). Additionally, Malachi 4:5 states that Elijah will be sent again by God to Israel "before the great and terrible day of the LORD."

These two individuals will arise probably during the first half of the tribulation. Like the prophets of the Old Testament, the two witnesses will be able to perform miracles.

They also will be protected by God against those who try to harm them before their mission is complete. For three-and-a-half years they will minister in Jerusalem without being harmed. At the end of the 1,260 days, God will remove their special protection. The Antichrist will then kill them, and their bodies will be left in the streets of Jerusalem for three-and-a-half days, after which God will resurrect them and rapture them to heaven. Once they have ascended to heaven, a great earthquake will occur, destroying a tenth of Jerusalem and killing 7,000 people.

The two witnesses will be clothed in sackcloth (Revelation 11:3), which is symbolic of the fact that they are prophets of doom (see Isaiah 37:1,2; Daniel 9:3). While Jerusalem is not mentioned by name as the city of their ministry, Revelation 11:8 says that their dead bodies will lie "in the street of the great city which mystically is called Sodom and Egypt, where also their Lord was crucified." The reference to the crucifixion clearly places these two witnesses in Jerusalem. The reference to Sodom and Egypt implies that, during this time, there will be licentious behavior and Jewish persecution in the city.

W

White Horse Judgment
See "Four Horsemen."

Whore of Babylon
The whore of Babylon is the King James Version term for the great harlot of Revelation 17:1,5ff.

See also "Harlot, Great."

Woes

First Woe   The book of Revelation speaks of three major judgments as "woes." The word *woe* is used in the Bible to refer to some great calamity usually seen as coming from the Lord, such as that pronounced by Christ upon Chorazin and Bethsaida in Matthew 11:21,22. The first woe is referenced in Revelation 9:12 and refers to the fifth trumpet judgment that has just past (Revelation 9:1-11).

Second Woe   The second woe is noted in Revelation 11:14 and is evidently a reference to Revelation 9:20,21. It involves the judgment at the end of the sixth trumpet, where Scripture speaks of great death and destruction upon the earth from which the rest of the "earth dwellers" would not repent.

Third Woe   The third woe is noted in Revelation 11:14 and refers to the seventh trumpet judgment which begins in Revelation 16:1. Since the seventh trumpet judgment includes the final seven bowl judgments, it must follow that the third woe encompasses all seven bowl judgments.

Z

Zechariah, Book of

The prophecy of Zechariah, written around 520–518 B.C., contains more about the coming Messiah than any other section except Isaiah. In the New Testament there are more than 40 citations of or allusions to the book. Zechariah prophesies of both the first and second coming of Christ. There is also extensive information and prophecy regarding Jerusalem during the tribulation and the millennial temple.

The primary prophetic focus of Zechariah relates to Jerusalem. It is not surprising to learn that *Zechariah* literally means "God remembers," which could be a response to Psalm 137. This psalm petitions earnestly for the Lord and fellow Jews not to forget Jerusalem: "If I forget you, O Jerusalem, may my right hand forget her skill. May my tongue cleave to the roof of my mouth, if I do not remember you, if I do not exalt Jerusalem above my chief joy" (verses 5,6).

Zechariah foretells the judgment and salvation of Israel and, specifically, of the city of Jerusalem. Chapter 8 speaks of the future of Jerusalem during the millennium. The book of Zechariah (14:16-21) concludes with a description of the millennium and its holy character. Dr. John Walvoord writes:

> The Book of Zechariah as a whole constituted one of the most compact apocalyptic prophetic books of the Old Testament. The Book of Zechariah included not only the eight prophetic dreams which were visions which occurred in one night (Zechariah 1:7–6:8) but also apocalyptic descriptions which constituted eschatological revelation. Chapters 9–14 concluded the book with two prophetic oracles relating to Israel's future restoration. Though the apocalyptic sections are not easy to interpret, careful study will reveal the literal

prophetic facts that are related to them (*Prophecy Knowledge Handbook*, p. 317).

The primary purpose of Zechariah's message was to comfort and console the weary nation of Israel. Along with the prophet Haggai, Zechariah strives to turn the nation back to God—and away from indifference and pursuits of personal pleasure. He tells the nation that even though they have forgotten God, God will not forget them. He foretells of a coming day of unparalleled glory (the millennium)—a day when the Messiah will personally rule the entire earth from Jerusalem.

Zion

The word *Zion* appears approximately 200 times in the Bible. Originally it referred to a rocky area between the Kidron Valley and Tyropoeon Valley of Jerusalem. Over time it came to mean all of "David's city." Apart from its geographical and historical meanings, the word has a threefold theological significance. First, it refers to David's city, Jerusalem. Jerusalem continues to be a city of international importance. Its prominence will not abate throughout the tribulation. Second, *Zion* is spoken of as the millennial city from which Jesus Christ will personally reign for a thousand years (see Isaiah 4:1-6; Zechariah 8:3-8). The mere use of *Zion* in certain biblical texts implies millennial overtones. It looks forward to the day when Messiah is finally seated on David's throne in the holy city, and all will be well with the world. Finally, *Zion* is used as a reference to the New Jerusalem, the heavenly city that will exist throughout eternity (Hebrews 12:22-24; Revelation 21; 22).

BIBLIOGRAPHY

Beechick, Allen. *The Pre-Tribulation Rapture*. Denver: Accent Books, 1980.

Benware, Paul N. *Understanding End Times Prophecy: A Comprehensive Approach*. Chicago: Moody Press, 1995.

Blackstone, William E. *Jesus Is Coming*. New York: Revell, 1898.

Boyer, James L. *Prophecy: Things to Come*. Winona Lake, IN: B.M.H. Books, 1973.

Brookes, James H. *Maranatha*. New York: Fleming H. Revell Company, 1889.

_____. *Till He Come*. New York: Fleming H. Revell Company, 1895.

Bultema, Harry. *Maranatha! A Study of Unfulfilled Prophecy*. Grand Rapids: Kregel Publications, 1985.

Campbell, Donald K., and Jeffrey L. Townsend. *A Case for Premillennialism*. Chicago: Moody Press, 1992.

Chafer, Lewis Sperry. *Systematic Theology*. 8 vols. Dallas: Dallas Seminary Press, 1947.

Couch, Mal, ed. *Dictionary of Premillennial Theology*. Grand Rapids: Kregel Publications, 1996.

Darby, J.N. *Will the Saints Be in the Tribulation?* New York: Loizeaux Brothers, n.d.

Demy, Timothy J., and Thomas D. Ice. "The Rapture and an Early Medieval Citation." *Bibliotheca Sacra* 152 (July–September 1995): 306-17.

Duty, Guy. *Escape from the Coming Tribulation*. Minneapolis: Bethany Fellowship, 1975.

Dyer, Charles H. *The Rise of Babylon: Sign of the End Times*. Wheaton, IL: Tyndale House Publishers, 1991.

_____. *World News and Bible Prophecy*. Wheaton, IL: Tyndale House Publishers, 1991.

English, E. Schuyler. *Re-Thinking the Rapture*. Neptune, NJ: Loizeaux Brothers, 1954.

Feinberg, Charles L. *Millennialism: The Two Major Views*. 4th ed. Chicago: Moody Press, 1980.

_____. *The Prophecy of Ezekiel.* Chicago: Moody Press, 1969.

Feinberg, Paul D. "The Case for the Pretribulation Rapture Position" in Richard R. Reiter, Paul D. Feibberg, Gleason L. Archer, Douglas J. Moo, *The Rapture: Pre-, Mid-, or Post- Tribulational?* Grand Rapids: Academie Books, 1984.

Fruchtenbaum, Arnold G. *Footsteps of the Messiah: A Study of the Sequence of Prophetic Events.* Tustin, CA: Ariel Press, 1982.

_____. *Israelology: The Missing Link in Systematic Theology.* Tustin, CA: Ariel Ministries Press, 1993.

_____. "The Nationality of the Anti-Christ." Englewood Cliffs, NJ: American Board of Missions to the Jews, n.d.

Harrison, Everett F. *Baker's Dictionary of Theology.* Grand Rapids: Baker Book House, 1960.

Harrison, William K. *Hope Triumphant: The Rapture of the Church.* Chicago: Moody Press, 1966.

Hindson, Ed. *Final Signs: Amazing Prophecies of the End Times.* Eugene, OR: Harvest House Publishers, 1996.

Hoehner, Harold W. *Chronological Aspects of the Life of Christ.* Grand Rapids: Zondervan Publishing House, 1977.

_____. "The Progression of Events in Ezekiel 38–39" in *Integrity of Heart, Skillfulness of Hands,* Charles H. Dyer and Roy B. Zuck, eds., pp. 82–91. Grand Rapids: Baker Books, 1994.

House, H. Wayne, and Thomas Ice. *Dominion Theology: Blessing or Curse?* Portland, OR: Multnomah Press, 1988.

Hoyt, Herman A. *The End Times.* Chicago: Moody Press, 1969.

Hullinger, Jerry. "The Problem of Animal Sacrifices in Ezekiel 40–48." *Bibliotheca Sacra* 152 (July–September 1995): 279-89.

Hunt, Dave. *A Cup of Trembling: Jerusalem and Bible Prophecy.* Eugene, OR: Harvest House Publishers, 1995.

Ice, Thomas, and Timothy Demy. *The Coming Cashless Society.* Eugene, OR: Harvest House Publishers, 1996.

_____. *The Truth About 2000 A.D. and Predicting Christ's Return,* Pocket Prophecy Series. Eugene, OR: Harvest House Publishers, 1996.

_____. *The Truth About the Antichrist and His Kingdom,* Pocket Prophecy Series. Eugene, OR: Harvest House Publishers, 1996.

_____. *The Truth About Armageddon and the Middle East,* Pocket Prophecy Series. Eugene, OR: Harvest House Publishers, 1997.

_____. *The Truth About Heaven and Eternity,* Pocket Prophecy Series. Eugene, OR: Harvest House Publishers, 1997.

_____. *The Truth About Jerusalem in Bible Prophecy,* Pocket Prophecy Series. Eugene, OR: Harvest House Publishers, 1996.

_____. *The Truth About the Millenium,* Pocket Prophecy Series. Eugene, OR: Harvest House Publishers, 1996.

_____. *The Truth About the Rapture,* Pocket Prophecy Series. Eugene, OR: Harvest House Publishers, 1996.

_____. *The Truth About Signs of the Times,* Pocket Prophecy Series. Eugene, OR: Harvest House Publishers, 1997.

_____. *The Truth About the Tribulation,* Pocket Prophecy Series. Eugene, OR: Harvest House Publishers, 1996.

_____, eds., *When the Trumpet Sounds: Today's Foremost Authorities Speak Out on End-Time Controversies.* Eugene, OR: Harvest House Publishers, 1995.

Ice, Thomas, and Randall Price. *Ready to Rebuild: The Imminent Plan to Rebuild the Last Days' Temple.* Eugene, OR: Harvest House Publishers, 1992.

Ironside, H.A. *Not Wrath, but Rapture.* New York: Loizeaux Brothers, 1946.

LaHaye, Tim. *No Fear of the Storm: Why Christians Will Escape All the Tribulation.* Portland, OR: Multnomah Press, 1992.

Larkin, Clarence. *Dispensational Truth.* Philadelphia: published privately, 1920.

Larsen, David L. *Jews, Gentiles, and the Church: A New Perspective on History and Prophecy.* Grand Rapids: Discovery House, 1995.

Lindsey, Hal. *The Rapture: Truth or Consequences?* New York: Bantam Books, 1983.

Lindsey, Hal, with C.C. Carlson. *The Late Great Planet Earth.* Grand Rapids: Zondervan Publishing House, 1970.

Mayhue, Richard L. *Snatched Before the Storm? A Case for Pretribulationism.* Winona Lake, IN: B.M.H. Books, 1980.

McClain, Alva J. *The Greatness of the Kingdom: An Inductive Study of the Kingdom of God.* Winona Lake, IN: B.M.H. Books, 1959.

Pache, René. *The Return of Jesus Christ.* Chicago: Moody Press, 1975.

Pember, G.H. *Great Prophecies of the Bible.* 4 vols. Reprint ed. Miami Springs, FL: Conely and Schoettle Publishers, 1984.

Pentecost, J. Dwight. *Things to Come: A Study in Biblical Eschatology.* Grand Rapids: Zondervan Publishing House, 1958.

_____. *Thy Kingdom Come.* Wheaton, IL: SP Publications, Inc., 1990.

Peters, George N.H. *The Theocratic Kingdom.* 3 vols. Grand Rapids: Kregel Publications, 1884.

Price, Randall. *In Search of Temple Treasures.* Eugene, OR: Harvest House Publishers, 1994.

Ryrie, Charles C. *Basic Theology.* Wheaton, IL: SP Publications, Inc. 1986.

_____. *The Basis of the Premillennial Faith.* Neptune, NJ: Loizeaux Brothers, 1953.

_____. *Come Quickly, Lord Jesus: What You Need to Know About the Rapture.* Eugene, OR: Harvest House Publishers, 1996.

_____. *Dispensationalism*. Chicago: Moody Press, 1995.

_____. *The Ryrie Study Bible*. Expanded edition. Chicago: Moody Press, 1995.

Schaff, Philip. *History of the Christian Church*. VIII vols., New York: Charles Scribner's Sons, 1882–1910.

Scofield, C.I. *Will the Church Pass Through the Great Tribulation?* Philadelphia: Philadelphia School of the Bible, 1917.

Showers, Renald. *Maranatha: Our Lord, Come!* Bellmawr, NJ: The Friends of Israel Gospel Ministry, 1995.

_____. *There Really Is a Difference! A Comparison of Covenant and Dispensational Theology*. Bellmawr, NJ: The Friends of Israel Gospel Ministry, 1990.

Stanton, Gerald B. *Kept from the Hour: Biblical Evidence for the Pretribulational Return of Christ*. 4th ed. Miami Springs, FL: Schoettle Publishing Co., 1991.

Stewart, Don, and Chuck Missler. *The Coming Temple: Center Stage for the Final Countdown*. Orange, CA: Dart Press, 1991.

Strombeck, J.F. *First the Rapture*. Eugene, OR: Harvest House Publishers, 1982.

Tan, Paul Lee. *The Interpretation of Prophecy*. Dallas: Bible Communications, Inc., 1974.

Thiessen, Henry C. *Will the Church Pass Through the Tribulation?* New York: Loizeaux Brothers, 1941.

Thomas, Robert L. *Revelation: An Exegetical Commentary*. 2 vols. Chicago: Moody Press, 1995.

Townsend, Jeffrey L. "Is the Present Age the Millennium?" in *Vital Prophetic Issues: Examining Promises and Problems in Eschatology*, pp. 68–82. Edited by Roy B. Zuck. Grand Rapids: Kregel Publications, 1995.

Walvoord, John F. *Armageddon, Oil and the Middle East Crisis*. Zondervan Publishing House, 1990.

_____. *The Blessed Hope and the Tribulation*. Grand Rapids: Zondervan Publishing House, 1976.

_____. *The Church in Prophecy*. Grand Rapids: Zondervan Publishing House, 1964.

_____. *Daniel: The Key to Prophetic Revelation*. Chicago: Moody Press, 1971.

_____. *Israel in Prophecy*. Grand Rapids: Zondervan Publishing House, 1964.

_____. *Major Bible Prophecies: 37 Crucial Prophecies That Affect You Today*. Grand Rapids: Zondervan Publishing House, 1991.

_____. *The Millennial Kingdom*. Findlay, OH; Dunham Publishing Company, 1959.

_____. *The Nations in Prophecy*. Grand Rapids: Zondervan Publishing House, 1967.

_____. *Prophecy: 14 Essential Keys to Understanding the Final Drama.* Nashville: Thomas Nelson Publishers, 1993.

_____. *The Prophecy Knowlecge Handbook.* Wheaton, IL: SP Publications, Inc., 1990.

_____. *The Rapture Question.* Grand Rapids: Zondervan Publishing House, 1979.

_____. *The Return of the Lord.* Grand Rapids: Zondervan Publishing House, 1955.

_____. *The Revelation of Jesus Christ.* Chicago: Moody Press, 1963.

Walvoord, John F., and Roy B. Zuck, eds. *The Bible Knowledge Commentary.* 2 vols. Wheaton, IL: Victor Books, 1985.

West, Nathaniel. *The Thousand Year Reign of Christ: The Classic Work on the Millennium.* Grand Rapids: Kregel Publications, 1993.

Willis, Wesly R., and John R. Master, and Charles C. Ryrie, eds. *Issues in Dispensationalism.* Chicago: Moody Press, 1994.

Willmington, Harold L. *Willmington's Guide to the Bible.* Wheaton, IL: Tyndale House Publishers, 1986.

Wood, Leon. *Is the Rapture Next?* Grand Rapids: Zondervan Publishing House, 1956.

Yamauchi, Edwin M. *Foes from the Northern Frontier.* Grand Rapids: Zondervan Publishing House, 1982.

Zuck, Roy B. *Basic Bible Interpretation.* Wheaton, IL: SP Publications, Inc., 1991.

ABOUT THE AUTHORS

Thomas Ice is director of the Pre-Trib Research Center and pastor of Trinity Bible Church in Fredricksburg, VA. He is a frequent radio and conference speaker and author of numerous books and articles on theology and prophetic issues. He coauthored *Ready to Rebuild*, The Pocket Prophecy Series, and *Dominion Theology: Blessing or Curse?* and coedited *When the Trumpet Sounds.* He has also contributed articles in *Issues in Dispensationalism,* the *Dictionary of Premillennial Theology,* and is a contributor to *The Nelson Study Bible.*

Before assuming his present postion, Ice pastored for 14 years in Oklahoma and Texas and served as a chaplain in the National Guard. He received his B.A. from Howard Payne University, a Th.M. in Historical Theology from Dallas Theological Seminary, a Ph.D. from Tyndale Theological Seminary. He and his wife, Janice, have been married 25 years and have three sons, Daniel, Timmy, and David.

Timothy Demy is a military chaplain presently assigned in Newport, R.I. He co-authored the Pocket Prophecy Series and co-edited *When the Trumpet Sounds* and *Suicide: A Christian Response* among others. His writings have appeared in magazines and other books, including the *Dictionary of Premillennial Theology* and the *Dictionary of Evangelical Biography.*

Demy received his B.A. from Texas Christian University, and a Th.M. and Th.D. in Historical Theology from Dallas Theological Seminary. Additionally, he earned an M.A. in European History from the University of Texas at Arlington and an M.A. in Human Development from Salve Regina University. He is currently pursuing a Ph.D. in Humanities and Technology. He and his wife, Lyn, have been married 19 years.

For information, contact:

Pre-Trib Research Center
10400 Courthouse Road, Suite 241
Spotsylvania, VA 22553